CAMBRIDGE
UNIVERSITY PRESS

CAMBRIDGE ENGLISH
Language Assessment
Part of the University of Cambridge

C000259318

Cambridge English

OFFICIAL
PREPARATION MATERIAL

EXAM BOOSTER
WITHOUT ANSWER KEY

FOR KEY AND KEY FOR SCHOOLS

Comprehensive exam practice for students

Caroline Chapman and Susan White

Cambridge University Press
www.cambridge.org/elt

Cambridge English Language Assessment
www.cambridgeenglish.org

Information on this title: www.cambridge.org/9781316641804

© Cambridge University Press and UCLES 2017

First published 2017
20 19 18 17 16 15 14 13 12 11 10 9 8 7 6 5 4 3

Printed in Italy by Rotolito S.p.A.

A catalogue record for this publication is available from the British Library

ISBN 978-1-316-64180-4

Additional resources for this publication at www.cambridge.org/keybooster

CONTENTS

Map of the book 4

Worksheets

Reading and Writing Part 1 6

Reading and Writing Part 2 12

Reading and Writing Part 3 18

Reading and Writing Part 4 24

Reading and Writing Part 5 30

Reading and Writing Part 6 36

Reading and Writing Part 7 42

Reading and Writing Part 8 48

Reading and Writing Part 9 54

Listening Part 1 60

Listening Part 2 66

Listening Part 3 72

Listening Part 4 78

Listening Part 5 84

Speaking Part 1 90

Speaking Part 2 96

Think about it 102

Key topic lists 110

MAP OF THE BOOK AND EXAM OVERVIEW

Paper 1: Reading and Writing 1 hour 10 minutes	Worksheet 1	Worksheet 2	Worksheet 3
Reading and Writing Part 1 p6 Matching 5 questions 5 marks	**Daily life** Present simple and adverbs of frequency Daily routine questions	**Places and buildings** Places vocabulary Asking for and giving information	**Services** Services vocabulary Understanding signs and notices
Reading and Writing Part 2 p12 3-option multiple choice 5 questions 5 marks	**Shopping** Shopping vocabulary Costs and amounts	**Food and drink** Food and drink vocabulary Ordering in a restaurant	**House and home** Adjectives Basic furniture and prepositions
Reading and Writing Part 3 p18 3-option multiple choice AND matching 10 questions 10 marks	**Social interaction** Questions Responding to invitations	**Feelings, opinions and experiences** Present perfect + *just, yet, already, never, ever, for* and *since*	**Hobbies and leisure** Hobbies vocabulary Arranging a social activity
Reading and Writing Part 4 p24 3-option multiple choice OR Right/Wrong/Doesn't say 7 questions 7 marks	**The natural world** Landscape vocabulary Expressing agreement and disagreement	**Education and study** School subjects vocabulary Past simple and past events	**Travel and holidays** Travel vocabulary Directions
Reading and Writing Part 5 p30 3-option multiple choice cloze 8 questions 8 marks	**Sports and games** *go, play* and *do* Past simple and past continuous	**Entertainment and media** Music vocabulary Suggesting, accepting and refusing	**Transport** Comparatives and superlatives Making predictions
Reading and Writing Part 6 p36 Spelling 5 questions 5 marks	**The weather** Letters and pronunciation Talking about the weather	**Clothes** Things to wear Pronouns	**People** Describing people Adjectives describing people
Reading and Writing Part 7 p42 Open cloze 10 questions 10 marks	**Daily life** Present simple and daily routine Email describing typical day	**Social interaction** Modals: possibility, ability and permission Present continuous and time expressions	**Travel and holidays** Past simple: irregular verbs Talking about future plans
Reading and Writing Part 8 p48 Information transfer 5 questions 5 marks	**Hobbies and leisure** Understanding short messages Expressing preferences	**Sport and activities** Sports vocabulary Completing a form with personal details	**Food and drink** Food groups Food preparation verbs
Reading and Writing Part 9 p54 Guided writing 1 question 5 marks	**Health and exercise** Mixed tenses Writing an email	**Personal identification** Family vocabulary Giving personal information	**Entertainment and media** Entertainment vocabulary Using punctuation

Paper 2: Listening About 30 minutes	Worksheet 1	Worksheet 2	Worksheet 3
Listening Part 1 p60 3-option multiple choice 5 questions 5 marks	**Services and places** Times, days and dates Places in town vocabulary	**Shopping and numbers** Numbers Shopping vocabulary	**Education and study** Present, future and past actions Daily routine
Listening Part 2 p66 Matching 5 questions 5 marks	**Food and drink** *this*, *that*, *these* and *those* Countable and uncountable	**Hobbies and shopping** Offers and requests Likes and preferences	**Countries and sports** Languages and nationalities Suggestions and responding
Listening Part 3 p72 3-option multiple choice 5 questions 5 marks	**Leisure time** Giving information about days, dates, times and prices Free time vocabulary	**Social media and technology** Digital world vocabulary Present and past simple passive	**Travel and holidays** Documents and texts vocabulary Talking about future plans
Listening Part 4 p78 Gap-fill 5 questions 5 marks	**Making plans** Time vocabulary and prepositions of time *Going to* and *will*	**Health, medicine and exercise** Parts of the body vocabulary Modals of advice	**Dates and services** Dates, months and events Giving the time, day or date
Listening Part 5 p84 Gap-fill 5 questions 5 marks	**House and home** Home vocabulary Word order in questions	**Entertainment and media** Taking down and giving phone numbers Imperatives	**Education and study** Expressing rules Modals of obligation
Paper 3: Speaking 8–10 minutes	Worksheet 1	Worksheet 2	Worksheet 3
Speaking Part 1 p90 Examiner asks questions 5–6 minutes	**Personal identification** Giving information about yourself Family vocabulary	**Daily life** Time expressions Word order and adverbs of frequency	**Places and buildings** Places in town vocabulary Talking about places you go to
Speaking Part 2 p96 Candidates exchange information 3-4 minutes	**Hobbies and leisure** Giving information about routines Seasons and months	**Sport** Action verbs Present simple questions	**Holidays and travel** Transport vocabulary Mixed tenses

Think about it p102

Key topic lists p110

Go to http://www.cambridgeenglish.org/exams/general-english-and-for-schools/ for useful information about preparing for the *Cambridge English: Key* and *Key for Schools* exams.

Daily life

☑ Exam task

1

Which notice (A–H) says this (1–5)? For questions (1–5), write the correct answer.

1. You can have this meal at any time.

2. You can only leave your car here in the afternoon or evening.

3. This place is cheaper in the evening.

4. There is someone here to help all day and night.

5. You must get to this place early.

A *Travel information office*
<u>Open 24 hours</u>

B Please arrive at least
10 minutes before
the time of your appointment.

C Staff restaurant
*Sorry – we've closed
early this afternoon.
Open normal time tomorrow.*

D <u>NO PARKING</u>
between midnight and midday.

E **Drive-through restaurant**
*Open Thursday, Friday
and Saturday 8 pm to midnight*

F **CAFÉ**
Our popular breakfasts
are available all day
at excellent prices!

G **SHORT-STAY CAR PARK**
£2.50 for two hours

H All drinks half-price
AFTER 5 PM.

2a

Put the adverbs in the box in the correct order, from the most frequent (5) to the least frequent (1).

sometimes .... never .... often ....
always .... usually ....

2b

Rewrite the sentences with the words or expressions in brackets in the correct place.

1. I have a meeting with my boss. (weekly)

....

2. My brother plays tennis. (once a week)

....

3. Do you have breakfast? (always)

....

4. I drive to work. (every day)

....

5. I visit my sister at the weekend. (often)

....

6. I go to bed before midnight. (never)

....

7. My family eat dinner at 6 pm. (usually)

....

8. I have lunch at my desk. (sometimes)

....

3a **Write the questions.**

1. time | usually | get up? ....

2. get up | different | time | at the weekend? ....

3. what | eat | for breakfast? ....

4. how | get | university? ....

5. time | lessons | start? ....

6. where | have | lunch? ....

7. how many | lessons | each day? ....

8. time | get | home? ....

9. what | usually | do | evening? ....

10. time | go | bed? ....

3b **Write your answers to five questions from Activity 3a. Use adverbs of frequency.**

1. ....

2. ....

3. ....

4. ....

5. ....

☑ *Exam facts*

- In this part, you read seven short texts. These are usually signs or notices.
- There are also five sentences.
- For each sentence, you have to choose the text that means the same thing.
- There are three texts that you don't need.

Places and buildings

1 Read the descriptions. Choose the correct answer, a, b or c.

1. You go here if you want to catch a plane.
   a station   **b** airport   **c** motorway

2. People go here to watch sports such as football.
   a roundabout   **b** theatre   **c** stadium

3. You can park your car in one of these.
   a garage   **b** lift   **c** underground

4. Businessmen and businesswomen work at desks in this place.
   a elevator   **b** pharmacy   **c** office

5. Parents take their children here so they can have fun.
   a playground   **b** market   **c** car park

6. Doctors and nurses work in this place.
   a guest-house   **b** hospital   **c** factory

7. You can study lots of different subjects in this place.
   a college   **b** supermarket   **c** hotel

8. People work in this place and make things such as cars.
   a museum   **b** cafeteria   **c** factory

☑ **Exam task**

2 Which notice (A–H) says this (1–5)?
For questions (1–5), write the correct answer.

1. Everyone needs to wear a hat in this place.

2. Speak to this person if you would like to work here.

3. You can only go out this way if you work here.

4. To get to other floors, you need to walk.

5. You should not take these with you when you go out.

A
> **Swimming pool**
> Take off shoes please!
> Children don't need hats in pool

B
> **Lift not working**
> *Please use stairs*

C
> **Guests**
> Give room keys to receptionist
> before leaving the hotel

D
> Door on this floor for staff only
> **NO EXIT FOR VISITORS**

E
> Factory staff and visitors
> Keep hair covered at all times

F
> **Visitors**
> Walk this way around the top
> floor of the castle

G
> SPORTS CENTRE
> New staff needed. Phone
> manager for more information.

H
> *Please do not make calls*
> while in the hospital building

Complete the dialogue with your own words. Put ONE word in each space.

Receptionist: Good morning. Can I
(1) .... you?

Nikki: Yes please. I **(2)** .... love to go to a museum. Is there one **(3)** .... this hotel?

Receptionist: Yes. You can walk to it from here. Just go out of the hotel, **(4)** .... left, walk for about ten minutes, and you will see it on your right.

Nikki: Thank you. **(5)** .... it a big museum?

Receptionist: Yes, it's the national museum. It's very large, and there's a lot to see there.

Nikki: That's great. I want to buy some postcards. **(6)** .... the museum have a shop?

Receptionist: Yes, it has a very nice shop. It **(7)** .... books, and gifts – and postcards, of course.

Nikki: Thank you very much for your help.

Receptionist: You're **(8)** .... ! Just ask me if you need anything else while you're staying here.

 Exam tips

- Quickly read the seven short texts and think about where you might see them.
- Look for words or phrases in the sentences and the short texts that have the same meaning.
- Compare each sentence with each text before you choose an answer.

Services

1 Complete the sentences below using words from the box.

bank	café	chemist	dentist	hotel
library	post office	tourist information		

1. I'm going to the .... to buy a stamp.
2. Is the .... open today? I need to get some cash.
3. My tooth hurts. I think I should make an appointment with my ....
4. I'm going to the .... to borrow a book about insects.
5. I've got my flight, but I still need to book a room in a .... for my holiday.
6. Is there a .... near here? I need to buy some medicine.
7. I booked a tour of the city at the .... centre.
8. Let's go to that new .... They make great hot chocolate.

2 Read the signs. Put the number in the correct part of the table.

Bank	Tourist information centre	Library
....	....	....

1 Please try to return books to the correct shelf. Thank you.

5 DVDs £1.50 for one week.

2 Need to find a room in a hotel? We can book one for you.

6 Computer course for beginners. Starts Monday.

3 Information about train and bus times at this desk only.

7 Lost your credit card? Call this number immediately. ☎ 970097 86809

4 Need to borrow money today? Speak to a member of staff.

8 Please pay for maps in cash.

 **Exam task**

3 Which notice (A–H) says this (1–5)?

For questions (1–5), write the correct answer.

1. Speak to this person if you want to know how much you will pay.
2. You don't have to pay for information at this place.
3. Be careful that you have enough money for this.
4. You have to pay if you don't take these back at the right time.
5. Customers can't pay with credit cards here.

A

> **Cinema**
> We cannot change your seats after you've paid for tickets.

B

> **Library members**
> *It will cost you £1 for books you return late.*

C

> **Tourist Office**
> Free maps and guidebooks – come inside and ask.

D

> **DENTIST**
> Ask the receptionist for our price list.

E

> **Post office**
> You can pay bills here. Ask staff for more information.

F

> **Café**
> Cash only at this desk, please.

G

> TOURISTS
> Need dollars or euros?
> Buy them here – cash or credit cards

H

> *Petrol station*
> Make sure you can pay before filling your car!

 **Get it right!**

Look at the sentence below. Then try to correct the mistake.

The weather is very beautiful and I stay often on the beach.

Shopping

1 Read the definitions. Then put the letters in the right order to make words.

1. This is how much you have to pay for something in a shop. (cirpe) ....
2. This is a piece of paper which you can use to pay for things. (hecequ) ....
3. This is a big shop which sells food and lots of other things. (mersteparuk) ....
4. This is what some people call a shop. (roset) ....
5. This word means something which is not cheap. (pivenexes) ....
6. This is a person who buys something in a shop. (turemocs) ....
7. If there is a problem with something you buy, you might do this with it. (gnecah) ....
8. If a shop isn't open 24 hours a day, it does this at night. (selco) ....

 **Exam task**

2 Read the sentences about a woman who goes shopping. Choose the best word (A, B or C) for each space.

1. Reena would like a new pair of jeans but she doesn't want to .... too much money.
   A spend   **B** cost   **C** save

2. Reena goes into a clothes shop, and the shop .... shows her some jeans.
   A staff   **B** colleague   **C** assistant

3. Reena decides to .... on the jeans in the changing room.
   A try   **B** get   **C** turn

4. Reena likes the jeans, and is happy because they are on ....
   A discount   **B** sale   **C** market

5. Reena pays for the jeans, and asks for her ....
   A list   **B** document   **C** receipt

3a 🔊 Track 1 **Listen to the conversations. Answer the questions with a price or number from the box. You do not need all of the prices and numbers.**

10	£3	4	£12	£4.50	6	200
£11.50	£15	3	£4	2	£1.50	

1. How much does the woman need to pay? ....
2. How much does the man need to pay? ....
3. How many pens does the woman buy? ....
4. How many calendars does the man buy? ....
5. How many bottles does the woman want to buy? ....
6. How much is one kilo of cheese? ....
7. How many plates does the woman buy? ....
8. How much did the man pay for his book? ....

3b **Write a few sentences about your favourite shop or shopping centre.**

....
....
....
....
....
....
....
....
....
....
....

☑ **Exam facts**

- In this part, you read five sentences about the same topic or story.
- Each sentence has one word missing.
- You have to choose one word (A, B or C) to complete each sentence.

© Cambridge University Press and UCLES 2015

Food and drink

1a Complete the text with the correct alternatives.

Breakfast around the world

Most people agree that it is important to eat breakfast in the morning. But breakfast is different all over the world. In Japan, for example, many people have a bowl of hot **(1)** *sauce / soup* for breakfast, but in Australia most people eat cold **(2)** *cereal / dessert* with milk. Milk is used to make **(3)** *omelette / yogurt*, which lots of Americans eat in the morning. **(4)** *Curry / Coffee* is a very popular breakfast drink, and in many countries people eat toast, which is **(5)** *grilled / fried* bread, with butter. In some European countries such as Germany and Sweden, people eat cold meats such as **(6)** *ham / burger* with their bread, or sometimes cheese, but in the UK people prefer something sweet such as **(7)** *jam / juice* on their toast at breakfast time. In countries where people cook in the morning, **(8)** *cakes / eggs* are very popular, and lots of people eat them with sausages.

1b Write a few sentences about breakfast in your country.

....
....
....
....
....
....
....
....
....

2

Read the sentences about a student who works in a restaurant.
Choose the best word (A, B or C) for each space.

1. Franz speaks to each customer and writes their .... in his notebook.
   A order   **B** menu   **C** sign

2. Sometimes Franz needs to .... to customers what is in the dishes.
   A understand   **B** decide   **C** explain

3. The restaurant chef tries to .... the food as quickly as possible.
   A prepare   **B** improve   **C** cover

4. When the food is ready, Franz .... it to the customers.
   A leaves   **B** serves   **C** puts

5. When the customers finish eating, they ask Franz for their ....
   A price   **B** bill   **C** purse

3

Read the phrases below, and decide who is speaking. Write W (waitress) or C (customer).

1. Excuse me, could I have some more water, please? ....
2. How would you like your steak cooked, sir? ....
3. That dish comes with salad or chips. Which would you prefer? ....
4. My food is cold! Is yours okay? ....
5. I think I'm going to have a dessert. They're really good here. ....
6. Shall I take your plates now? ....
7. Could you ask the chef to make my pizza without onions, please? ....
8. Good evening. We've booked a table for six people. ....

☑ **Exam tips**

- Look at the words before and after each space.
- Try each word (A, B and C) in the space before choosing the correct answer.
- When you have completed the five sentences, read them all again to make sure they make sense.

House and home

1

Sort the words in the box into three groups. Give each group a title.

golden	large	pale pink	purple
round	small	square	star

Group 1	Group 2	Group 3 ....
....	....	....
....	....	....
....	....	....

☑ **Exam task**

2

Read the sentences about Samira's new house.
Choose the best word (A, B or C) for each space.

1. Samira's family have taken all of their .... , like sofas, to the new house.
   A luggage   **B** furniture   **C** software

2. In their old house, Samira .... a bedroom with her sister, but now she has her own bedroom.
   A included   **B** joined   **C** shared

3. Samira has put all of her things in the drawers and ....
   A cupboards   **B** shelves   **C** carpets

4. The light in Samira's room is broken, but her father says he can .... it.
   A build   **B** repair   **C** improve

5. Samira has decided to .... her new room in her favourite colour, green.
   A print   **B** fill   **C** paint

 **Get it right!**

Look at the sentences below and choose the correct one.

Today we went to visit the Tower and last night we had a nice meal at my friend's house.

Today we went to visit the Tower and last night we had a nice meal in my friend's house.

3a Look at the picture of a living room. Are the sentences TRUE or FALSE?

1. There is a table between the two armchairs. ....
2. There are three black chairs around the long table. ....
3. There is a mirror between the two large windows. ....
4. One of the tables has a bowl of fruit on it. ....
5. There is a book next to the plant. ....
6. There is a lamp in the corner of the room. ....
7. The television is on the wall, near one of the windows. ....
8. There is a carpet in front of the sofa. ....

3b Write a few sentences about your living room.

....

....

....

....

....

....

....

....

....

....

Social interaction

1 Complete the questions with the correct question word(s).

1. .... is that, sitting near the door?
2. .... do you come here? Once a week?
3. .... bag is that, on the chair?
4. .... song shall we listen to first?
5. .... have you lived here?

6. .... do you think we should do?
7. .... did you buy that hat? I'd like to get one.
8. .... will we see you again?

☑ Exam facts

- This part of the test has two tasks.
- In the first task, you read what someone says, and you have to choose one reply (A, B or C) to complete the conversation.
- In the second task, you read what one person says in a longer conversation, and you have to choose the second person's replies.

© Cambridge University Press and UCLES 2015

☑ Exam task

2 Complete the five conversations.
For questions 1–5, choose A, B or C.

1. I'm sorry I didn't come to your party.
   - **A** Yes, you are.
   - **B** That's okay.
   - **C** Did you?

2. Can you help me with this heavy bag, please?
   - **A** I think it's mine.
   - **B** No, it isn't.
   - **C** Yes, of course.

3. I'm from Italy.
   - **A** What's it like?
   - **B** Is it yours?
   - **C** Yes, you're right.

4. Thanks for the lovely present.
   - **A** Oh, it's yours!
   - **B** If you're sure.
   - **C** You're welcome.

5. This is my friend Richard.
   - **A** That was nice of him.
   - **B** Pleased to meet you.
   - **C** I think you should.

Now complete the conversation between two friends. What does Sofia say to Zoe?

For questions 6–10, choose the correct letter A–H.

Zoe: Hi Sofia. Have you got any plans for the weekend?

Sofia: No, nothing special.

Zoe: Oh. Well, shall we do something together?

Sofia: **6** ....

Zoe: Why don't you come to my house to watch a film on Saturday evening?

Sofia: **7** ....

Zoe: Thanks. Shall we ask some other people too?

Sofia: **8** ....

Zoe: And I think Ada might be able to come too. I'll ask her.

Sofia: **9** ....

Zoe: Why don't you come earlier than that?

Sofia: **10** ....

Zoe: I'm sure it will be! See you on Saturday then.

A So we can chat before the film? Is an hour enough?

B That's a good idea. See you at 8 o'clock?

C Doesn't she usually work at that time?

D There's a book I need to read for college, but nothing else.

E Yeah, I'd like that. Any ideas?

F I don't think we are.

G Sure. My sister's probably free.

H OK. I'll bring some snacks and drinks.

---

3 Pieter asks his friend Sami to come to his house for dinner. Tick (✓) the two polite responses to the question.

Pieter: Would you like to come to my house for dinner on Sunday, Sami?

Sami:

1. No, I can't. ☐

2. Thanks, that's a lovely idea. ☐

3. I'm afraid I'm busy then. ☐

4. No, I would not like to. ☐

Feelings, opinions and experiences

1 Put the words into the correct order to make sentences and questions.

1. Japan / been / to / never / have / I / .

....

2. here / she / worked / years / for / has / three / .

....

3. mountain / have / a / climbed / ever / you / ?

....

4. just / mum / have / I / seen / your / .

....

5. the / started / film / yet / has / ?

....

6. dinner / already / I / finished / have / my / .

....

7. for / we / lived / months / have / here / two / .

....

8. to / wanted / I / him / always / meet / have / !

....

☑ *Exam task*

2 Complete the five conversations.

For questions 1–5, choose A, B or C.

1. I met my new neighbour today!
   A What's she like?
   B Does she know?
   C Has she been there?

2. Did you have a good evening?
   A No, I don't think it was.
   B Yes, lovely, thank you.
   C Thanks, but I'm busy.

3. Where do you prefer to sit?
   A Is it on this side?
   B Yes, I think we should.
   C Near the window, please.

4. Have you ever been to the ballet?
   A There aren't any tickets.
   B It's a great idea!
   C Not until today!

5. I've never seen that boy before.
   A Shall I ask him?
   B I think he's new.
   C It isn't his.

Now complete the conversation between two friends.
What does Kim say to Serena?
For questions 6–10, choose the correct letter A–H.

Serena: Hi Kim! I haven't seen you for ages!

Kim: Yes, I know. It's been so long.

Serena: Have you been ill?

Kim: **6** ....

Serena: Oh, lucky you! Where did you go?

Kim: **7** ....

Serena: I didn't know that. Was it your first visit?

Kim: **8** ....

Serena: No, but I'd like to. When is the best time to go?

Kim: **9** ....

Serena: That's good to know. So, did you take any photos?

Kim: **10** ....

Serena: Yeah, I'd love that. Thanks.

A I did – in Thailand!

B Of course! I'll show them to you when you have some time.

C Probably when it's winter here.

D I was at home at the weekend.

E Yes, that's true. Not since last month.

F To Australia. My brother lives there.

G No! I was on holiday!

H Actually, I've been there before. Have you ever been?

---

3 ◀)) Track 2 **Listen to the conversations. Answer the questions.**

1. When will they go shopping? ....

2. Do the speakers agree with each other? ....

3. Does the man like his new phone? ....

4. What time will they leave? ....

5. Did the woman like the film? ....

6. What do they decide to eat? ....

7. What will the man wear? ....

8. Does the man prefer his laptop or the woman's laptop? ....

☑ *Exam tips*

- In the first task, read the first part of each conversation and think what the second person might say.
- Then look at options, A, B and C, and decide which one completes the conversation.
- In the second task, when choosing the correct option, look at the sentences before and after the gap.
- When you complete the conversations, read them again to make sure they make sense.

Hobbies and leisure

1 Complete these sentences with the correct word. The first letter of the word is given to help you.

1. A cinema is a place where people go to watch f ....
2. If you want to see a p .... you can go to a theatre.
3. My hobby is photography. I've just bought a new c................ .
4. My younger brother loves c................ and he wants to be a chef when he's older.
5. I'm going out for a m.......... tonight, to my favourite restaurant.
6. I'm interested in art. I often go to a m .... to look at paintings.
7. My friend spends a lot of time on his computer playing v .... games.
8. I play the piano. Do you play a musical i .... ?

☑ Exam task

2 Complete the five conversations.
For questions 1–5, choose A, B or C.

1. What did you think of that book?

   A I forgot to bring it.
   B It isn't mine.
   C I enjoyed it.

2. Shall we have a picnic?

   A I'd prefer a barbecue.
   B Yes, I think it might.
   C I'm going to a party.

3. Would you like a cup of tea?

   A Yes, I'd love to, thanks.
   B Coffee for me, please.
   C I like it a lot.

4. I prefer this car to your old one.

   A Have you?
   B That's it!
   C Me too!

5. Suzy doesn't like her new job.

   A That's a shame.
   B No, it isn't.
   C Oh, I do!

Now complete the conversation between two friends.

What does Malik say to Daniel?

For questions 6–10, choose the correct letter A–H.

Daniel: What do you like doing in your free time, Malik?

Malik: Well, I really like music.

Daniel: Yeah, me too. Do you ever go to concerts?

Malik: **6** ....

Daniel: Well, I'm going to one this Saturday. And it's free!

Malik: **7** ....

Daniel: Do you know the park near my house?

Malik: **8** ....

Daniel: That's it. There's going to be music, and food too. But you have to pay for the food!

Malik: **9** ....

Daniel: No, it's in the afternoon. It starts at 3 o'clock. Why don't you come with me and my friends?

Malik: **10** ....

Daniel: Yeah, that's fine. See you there.

A I think so. Is it behind the cinema?

B Of course! Is it in the evening?

C Maybe watch films. But I don't have much free time.

D I've never been there before.

E I read sometimes. And I play the guitar. I love music!

F Thanks. I'd like that. Shall I text you when I get to the park?

G They're usually too expensive for me.

H That sounds great. Where is it?

---

3 **Complete the sentences with the correct alternatives.**

1. I don't *mind / care* classical music, but I prefer pop.
2. I *nearly / quite* like art, especially modern art.
3. I enjoy playing music *most / more* than listening to it.
4. Jack *really / very* loves films, and goes to the cinema a lot.
5. Stan doesn't watch TV *many / much*. He prefers going out.
6. What's your *best / favourite* type of food?
7. Al doesn't *like / love* that new restaurant near his house at all.
8. I like camping – *also / even* when it rains.

⊙ **Get it right!**

Look at the sentence below. Then try to correct the mistake.

There are lots of things to see here, and I already saw the Statue of Liberty and the American Museum of Natural History.

The natural world

1 Match the words in the box to the correct definition.

desert	field	forest	island	lake	mountains	plants	river

1. a large area of water, often in a park ....
2. a very large area which has lots of trees in it ....
3. a piece of land with water all around it ....
4. trees and flowers are examples of these ....
5. a very dry area where it doesn't rain much ....
6. a long area of water that often ends in the sea ....
7. a farmer grows things or puts his animals here ....
8. these are very tall and often have snow at the top ....

☑ *Exam facts*

- In this part, you read a text – for example, a short newspaper or magazine article.
- You have to answer seven questions.
- These may be Right, Wrong, Doesn't say or A, B or C questions.

© Cambridge University Press and UCLES 2015

☑ *Exam task*

2 Read the article about three people who are interested in nature.
Answer the questions. For questions 1–7, choose A, B or C.

My love of nature

A   Sarah

When I was a child at school, I collected books about nature. My classmates and friends all spent their free time playing computer games, so to them I was a bit strange. I loved learning about animals from other countries, but as I got older I found out that my own country has interesting nature too, and that's what I like studying now. I do lots of drawings of nature, and I put them on my blog.

B   Pilar

I love birds and animals because of all the visits to forests and lakes we made when I was at school. It's a shame that things have changed now. Children these days don't learn enough about nature, so lots of them are afraid of insects, for example. I have a great job because of my love of nature. I'm a nature photographer. It's brilliant, except for the early mornings!

C   Lia

A few years ago I read a blog with beautiful photos of animals, birds and plants, which made me start really looking at what lives around us. It was just a hobby at first, but now it's my job as I visit schools and give talks about nature. I love it. The only problem is if I am asked to draw a picture. I enjoy it, but I'm terrible at drawing! I'm going to take some lessons to try to get better.

1. Who became interested in nature from seeing someone else's blog?

   A Sarah   **B** Pilar   **C** Lia

2. Who says there is something about her job that she doesn't like?

   A Sarah   **B** Pilar   **C** Lia

3. Whose friends thought that her hobby was unusual?

   A Sarah   **B** Pilar   **C** Lia

4. Who became interested in nature because of school trips?

   A Sarah   **B** Pilar   **C** Lia

5. Who says that the type of nature she is interested in has changed?

   A Sarah   **B** Pilar   **C** Lia

6. Who wants to improve her pictures of nature?

   A Sarah   **B** Pilar   **C** Lia

7. Who thinks that young people should learn more about nature at school?

   A Sarah   **B** Pilar   **C** Lia

3   **Complete the conversation with phrases from the boxes.**

Adam: Do you live in a town, Ben?

Ben: No, in the countryside. And I love it.

Adam: **(1)** .... I lived in the countryside when I was a child, but I prefer towns.

Ben: Oh! Why is that?

Adam: Well, in the countryside you're so far away from schools, shops and friends' houses.

Ben: **(2)** .... You get more exercise because you have to walk more!

Adam: **(3)** .... You spend a lot of time in your car, driving everywhere!

Ben: But the traffic is much worse in towns. Towns are too noisy and busy.

Adam: **(4)** .... The countryside is boring!

Ben: **(5)** .... You can go walking, cycling, fishing – there are lots of things to do!

Adam: Yes – I can do them during short visits to the countryside! But I prefer to live in a town.

Ben: **(6)** .... I'm sure the view from my window is better that yours.

Adam: You're probably right. It's true that the countryside is beautiful, but I enjoy being with lots of people.

Ben: And that's what I hate!

Adam: Everyone is different, I suppose.

Ben: We certainly are!

Ben	**Adam**
a No, it isn't.	**d** No, you don't.
b Yes, but that's a good thing.	**e** Really? I don't understand that.
c Well, I don't.	**f** That's what I like!

Education and study

1 Complete the text below with the school subjects. Use the letters in brackets to help you.

There are lots of different subjects you can study at university. If you are good at **(1)** .... (gauselnag), you may decide to study French, Arabic or Chinese. If you like learning about how things work, then you probably find science subjects such as **(2)** .... (gibyolo), **(3)** .... (myshecrit) or **(4)** .... (shycips) interesting. People who are interested in things which happened a long time ago should study **(5)** .... (osriyth), but if you prefer learning about rivers, mountains and the different countries of the world, then you should choose **(6)** .... (regopaygh). People who are good with numbers often decide to study **(7)** .... (shacamittem), and those who want to become doctors take a course in **(8)** .... (necmidei).

☑ Exam task

2 Read the article about a new type of school desk.

Answer the questions. For questions 1–7, choose A, B or C.

We know that sitting down all the time is bad for us, and for this reason, standing desks have become quite popular in offices. A 'standing desk' is higher than a normal desk, so that people can do their work standing up. Now, schools are starting to use them too. Over the last few years, students in schools all over the world have tried these desks. But students don't have to stand for the whole school day, because standing desks come with stools – high chairs without backs – so they can sit down when they want to.

Teachers at a school in the US which tried the standing desks say that students listened to the teacher more during lessons when they used the desks. The teachers were surprised to see that younger students used the stools less than the older students. They think that this is because older students have already spent years sitting at desks, so it is difficult for them to change what they do.

So will all schools start using standing desks soon? Well, they aren't cheap, so most schools will probably use their old desks for quite a few more years first.

1. Standing desks are taller than normal desks.

   A Right   **B** Wrong   **C** Doesn't say

2. More offices than schools use standing desks.

   A Right   **B** Wrong   **C** Doesn't say

3. Standing desks have been tried in only one country.

   A Right   **B** Wrong   **C** Doesn't say

4. If a class use standing desks, the teacher tells the students when to sit down.

   A Right   **B** Wrong   **C** Doesn't say

5. Students who use standing desks work better in groups.

   A Right   **B** Wrong   **C** Doesn't say

6. Older students like sitting down at desks more than younger students.

   A Right   **B** Wrong   **C** Doesn't say

7. Standing desks are less expensive than normal desks.

   A Right   **B** Wrong   **C** Doesn't say

3

Complete the sentences with the correct alternatives.

1. I *broken / break / broke* my pen yesterday.

2. When I was little I didn't *known / know / knew* how to write.

3. I *ridden / rode / ride* my new bike to college yesterday.

4. I was so tired when I got home from school that I *lain / lie / lay* down and fell asleep.

5. I *took / taken / take* my exams last week.

6. We *given / give / gave* our teacher a present at the end of the year.

7. Did you *saw / see / seen* your friend at college?

8. I didn't *go / went / gone* to school until I was seven years old.

☑ *Exam tips*

- Quickly read the text before you answer the questions.

- The questions are in the same order as the information in the text.

- Compare the questions and options to the text carefully.

- Don't think an answer is right just because you see the same word in the text and the question.

Travel and holidays

1 Compete the advice about plane travel. The first letter of each word is given to help you.

If you are going to travel to a different country, you need to have a **(1)** p .... When you are packing, try not to put too much in your **(2)** l .... Try to get to the **(3)** a .... a few hours before your flight so that you won't **(4)** m .... it, and so that you get a good **(5)** s .... on the plane. Take something to read, as there may be a **(6)** d .... if the flight is late, or if the weather is bad. During the flight, be polite to other **(7)** p .... , and remember to listen to the instructions which the **(8)** p .... and other airline staff give you.

☑ *Exam tasks*

2 Read the article about three people's holidays.

Answer the questions. For questions 1–7, choose A, B or C.

My last holiday

A Max

I went on holiday with my friends. The flight was fine, but it took two hours by bus to reach the hotel – I didn't enjoy that! The hotel was noisy and the staff weren't friendly, but it didn't matter because we spent all our time on the beach, a short walk away. We tried lots of new dishes in the restaurants in the town. It was hard to sleep with such high temperatures, but we had a fantastic time, and the best thing was, we spent almost nothing once we arrived!

B Felipe

The drive to our hotel from the airport was along lovely country roads. The hotel my wife and I stayed in was quite expensive. The people who worked there were wonderful, but I wasn't so sure about the hotel restaurant – the desserts were fine, but the main courses weren't very good. It was cloudy and rainy most days, but we went to walk in the countryside, not to lie on a beach.

C Nikhil

My family and I drove across the USA last year. We stayed in lots of different hotels. I don't know how much we spent because my parents paid. There was a lot of driving, but my dad enjoyed that. The weather was fantastic, and I couldn't believe the differences in what people ate from place to place. It was good to be with the family, because there was always someone to talk to, or to do things with.

1. Who was surprised about the variety of food on holiday?

    A Max   **B** Felipe   **C** Nikhil

2. Who thought that part of their journey was too long?

    A Max   **B** Felipe   **C** Nikhil

3. Who liked travelling with a group of people?

    A Max   **B** Felipe   **C** Nikhil

4. Who was happy with the cost of their holiday?

    A Max   **B** Felipe   **C** Nikhil

5. Who thought the hotel staff were good?

    A Max   **B** Felipe   **C** Nikhil

6. Who was unhappy with some of the food they ate?

    A Max   **B** Felipe   **C** Nikhil

7. Who says that the weather was a problem at times?

    A Max   **B** Felipe   **C** Nikhil

3   🔊 **Track 3 Listen to the conversations. Are the sentences TRUE or FALSE?**

1. The woman needs to drive north to get to the airport. ....
2. The man needs to go straight on at the roundabout. ....
3. The restaurant is a long way from the hotel. ....
4. The man knows a faster way to get to the beach. ....
5. The man and the woman need to go south. ....
6. The man and the woman need to turn left to get to the market. ....
7. The hotel is on the road where the man already is. ....
8. The woman needs to turn right immediately. ....

🎯 *Get it right!*

Look at the sentence below. Then try to correct the mistake.

I've seen my brother yesterday.

Sports and games

1a Put the sports and games into the correct part of the table.

chess	exercise	fishing
football	golf	karate	skiing
swimming	tennis	

go	play	do

1b Look at the table. Are there any rules about which verb to use with which nouns? Can you add more sports or games to the table?

☑ Exam tasks

2 Read the article about tennis.

Choose the best word (A, B or C) for each space.

Tennis

The English name 'tennis' comes from the French word 'tenez', **(1)** .... means 'to hold'. When the first games of tennis **(2)** .... played hundreds of years ago, people used **(3)** .... hands to hit the ball. Now, of course, we use rackets.

A player **(4)** .... to get four points to win a game, and six games to win a set. In women's tennis, a player wins the match **(5)** .... winning two sets. This is often the same in men's tennis, **(6)** .... in some competitions men need to win three sets to win a match.

If two people play tennis against each **(7)** .... , it is called a singles match. If **(8)** .... are two players on each side, it is called a doubles match.

1	**A** who	**B** that	**C** which
2	**A** is	**B** were	**C** was
3	**A** their	**B** his	**C** your
4	**A** can	**B** must	**C** has
5	**A** by	**B** at	**C** for
6	**A** so	**B** but	**C** with
7	**A** one	**B** other	**C** own
8	**A** there	**B** here	**C** where

3a **Complete the sentences with the correct alternatives.**

1. When I *cycled / was cycling* in the park, I *saw / was seeing* Cristina.

2. I hurt my leg while I *played / was playing* football.

3. I *called / was calling* you at 8 o'clock last night, but you didn't answer. What *did you do / were you doing*?

4. We were so late for the match that they *already played / were already playing* when we arrived.

5. We *played / were playing* tennis when it started raining, so we *stopped / were stopping*.

6. *Did you go / Were you going* skiing when you were in Austria?

7. I *forgot / was forgetting* to bring my badminton racket, but Fay had two so she *lent / was lending* me one.

8. I *met / was meeting* a really interesting man when I *fished / was fishing* yesterday.

3b **Write a few sentences about a sport that you like.**

....
....
....
....
....
....
....
....
....
....

☑ **Exam facts**

- In this part, you read a short text – for example a newspaper or magazine article.

- There are eight missing words in the text.

- You have to choose the correct word (A, B or C) to complete each space.

Entertainment and media

1 Match the musical words with the definitions.

1.	To play this instrument you have to hit it.	**a**	practice
2.	A group of people who play music together.	**b**	opera
3.	A person who plays an instrument.	**c**	drum
4.	Lots of songs together by the same band or artist.	**d**	band
5.	You need to do this a lot when you learn to play an instrument.	**e**	album
6.	You touch the black and white parts of this instrument to play it.	**f**	record
7.	A musical play where people sing the words.	**g**	musician
8.	People do this with their music so that other people can listen to it.	**h**	keyboard

☑ Exam task

2 Read the article about a rock concert.

Choose the best word (A, B or C) for each space.

A rock concert

Famous groups don't come to my town very often, **(1)** .... when my brother showed me a poster for a concert by my favourite band, I was really excited. We asked some friends **(2)** .... they wanted to come with **(3)** .... , and then we bought the tickets.

A few weeks later, we met at my house and got a bus to the concert, **(4)** .... was in a stadium. We didn't know the first band who played – they weren't famous. Their music was okay, **(5)** .... not great. I just **(6)** .... wait for my favourite group to play. When they finally came onto the stage everyone started **(7)** .... They played all of their best songs, and of course the crowd all sang too. I don't think I will **(8)** .... forget that night.

1	**A** because		**B** so		**C** except
2	**A** if		**B** that		**C** as
3	**A** us		**B** them		**C** we
4	**A** what		**B** who		**C** which
5	**A** or		**B** but		**C** and
6	**A** shouldn't		**B** mustn't		**C** couldn't
7	**A** shout		**B** shouting		**C** shouted
8	**A** ever		**B** always		**C** never

3 Read the suggestions. Choose the TWO correct answers from a, b or c.

1. Why don't we go to a museum at the weekend?
   a I don't want to do that at all.
   b I'd prefer to go to a concert.
   c Okay, that sounds good.

2. Shall we have dinner together on Friday?
   a I'm busy then, but maybe another day?
   b I'm sorry, I'm busy then.
   c I don't think we will, no.

3. Let's watch a film.
   a No, let's not.
   b No, let's do something else.
   c No, not just at the moment.

4. How about going to a concert on Sunday?
   a Yes, I'd love to.
   b Yes, that's right.
   c Yes, that's a great idea.

5. Why don't you ask Maya to come to the opera?
   a I don't think she likes opera.
   b Because I don't like opera.
   c I might do that!

6. Shall we listen to some music?
   a Maybe later?
   b Yeah, lovely!
   c We shall not.

7. I'll take a photo, shall I?
   a No, don't worry.
   b No, you won't.
   c No, I'll do it.

8. Let's go dancing at the weekend.
   a Sure. Why not?
   b Why should we?
   c That's not a bad idea!

☑ Exam tips

- Quickly read the text before you choose your answers.
- Try each word (A, B and C) in the space before you choose the correct answer.
- Read the whole sentence carefully when you choose an answer.

Transport

1a Complete the table with the comparative and superlative forms of the adjectives.

adjective	comparative	superlative
big	....	....
bad	....	....
fast	....	....
dirty	....	....
modern	....	....
healthy	....	....
popular	....	....
crowded	....	....

1b Complete each sentence with a word from Exercise 1a.

1. The traffic is .... during the week than at weekends, because everyone is going to work.
2. Wow! I thought my car needed a wash, but yours is even .... than mine!
3. The trains in this city are the .... I've even been on. There are so many people on them!
4. I get home later in the evening now that I walk, but it's .... for me than driving.
5. There's a lot of space in this car – it's .... than the one you had before.
6. In cities which have a river, boats are quite a .... way to get around.
7. A hundred years ago, the .... car in the world could only travel at 136 km/h.
8. We have a lovely .... railway station now – much better than the old one.

☑ Exam task

2 Read the article about travelling by car.

Choose the best word (A, B or C) for each space.

Better ways to travel

Millions of us use our cars every day to get to work, college or school. Travelling by car is fast and comfortable, but not good for the world **(1)** .... us. So what **(2)** .... we do? One possibility is to share car journeys. If you have neighbours **(3)** .... travel to the same place, **(4)** .... together in one car. Two or three people travelling together is **(5)** .... than two or three cars making the same journey with only one person in **(6)** .... car.

Of course, cars are not the **(7)** .... way to travel. It's usually possible to make your journey by bus, tram or train, especially in a town or city. And if your journey is short, what **(8)** .... walking or going by bike? You'll get fit, and save money too!

1	**A** beside	**B** across	**C** around
2	**A** can	**B** would	**C** may
3	**A** what	**B** which	**C** who
4	**A** go	**B** gone	**C** going
5	**A** good	**B** better	**C** best
6	**A** other	**B** each	**C** any
7	**A** only	**B** single	**C** alone
8	**A** with	**B** to	**C** about

3a **Read the predictions about the future. Look at the <u>underlined</u> phrases and number them 1–5 (1 = most likely to happen, 5 = least likely to happen).**

a <u>I think</u> plane journeys will be shorter in the future. ....

b <u>It's possible</u> that / <u>Maybe</u> we'll all have flying cars in the future. ....

c <u>I'm very sure</u> / <u>I'm certain</u> that our journeys to work will be shorter, because trains are getting faster. ....

d <u>I'm not sure</u> if we'll still travel by train a hundred years from now. ....

e <u>I'm sure</u> we won't use petrol in our cars for much longer. ....

3b **Write five sentences about what you think will happen to transport in the future. Use the phrases from Exercise 3a.**

1. ....
2. ....
3. ....
4. ....
5. ....

Get it right!

Look at the sentences below and choose the correct one.

The most thing I like about it is the camera.

The thing I like most about it is the camera.

The weather

1 Put the letters of the English alphabet in the correct part of the table according to how they are pronounced.

/eɪ/	/iː/	/e/	/aɪ/	/oʊ/	/uː/	/ɑː/
a	b	f	i	o	q	r
h	c	l	_		_	
_	d	m			_	
_	e	n				
	_	_				
	_	_				
	_	_				
_						

☑ **Exam task**

2 Read the descriptions of some words about the weather.

What is the word for each one?

The first letter is already there. There is one space for each other letter in the word.

1. These are white, grey or black, and you can see them in the sky.   c _ _ _ _ _
2. When the weather is very cold, water changes to this.   i _ _
3. In this type of weather it is difficult to see where you are going.   f _ _ _ _
4. This is what the weather is like in the desert, because it doesn't rain much.   d _ _
5. During one of these it rains a lot and it is very windy.   s _ _ _ _

3a Match the comments about the weather to the replies.

1. It's going to be hot today.	**a** Me too. It's fun to play in.
2. The weather was great at the weekend.	**b** Really? Oh, I'll change my clothes then.
3. Do you think it'll rain later?	**c** No. I was asleep.
4. What's the weather like where you live?	**d** But it's so different today!
5. I love the snow!	**e** Yes, take your umbrella.
6. Did you hear the thunderstorm last night?	**f** It's warm and sunny here, as usual.

3b Write a few sentences about the weather in your country.

....
....
....
....
....
....
....
....
....
....

☑ Exam facts

- In this part, you read the descriptions of five words.
- You have to write the five words and spell them correctly.
- You can see the first letter of each word and the number of missing letters.

Clothes

1 Complete the table with the words from the box.

boots	cap	hat	shoes
shorts	tights	trainers	trousers

feet	head	legs
....	....	....
....	....	....
....		....

☑ **Exam task**

2 Read the descriptions of some words about clothes.

What is the word for each one?

The first letter is already there. There is one space for each other letter in the word.

1. This is often made of wool, and keeps you warm in cold weather.   **s** _ _ _ _ _ _
2. Your wear these on your hands.   **g** _ _ _ _ _
3. This covers your legs and is usually worn by women.   **s** _ _ _ _
4. This stops your trousers falling down.   **b** _ _ _
5. You wear this around your neck in cold weather.   **s** _ _ _ _

3a **Complete the sentences with the correct alternatives.**

1. Remy, is this scarf *you / your / yours* ?
2. *What / Who / Which* does this jumper belong to?
3. My cousin is only two, but she can already dress *herself / itself / yourself*.
4. I've brought a spare swimming costume, because I thought *someone / anyone / no one* might forget theirs.
5. I can't find my belt. Do you have *this / one / it* I can borrow?
6. I need to buy some ties for work. I don't have *many / much / more*.

3b **Write a few sentences about what you are wearing today.**

....

....

....

....

....

....

....

....

....

....

☑ Exam tips

- All the words are about the same topic. The instructions of the task tell you what the topic is.
- The answers are normally nouns. They are often singular, but some can be plural.
- Only write one letter in each space, and don't leave any spaces empty.

People

1 Read the definitions. Are the sentences TRUE or FALSE?

1. A beard is the hair on a man's face, under his mouth. ....
2. Someone who is fair has dark hair or skin. ....
3. Terrible means really good. ....
4. Horrible is used to describe something or someone which is not nice at all. ....
5. If someone is fun, other people like spending time with them. ....

☑ Exam task

2 Read the descriptions of some words used to describe people.

What is the word for each one?

The first letter is already there. There is one space for each other letter in the word.

1. This word is used for someone who isn't very tall.   s _ _ _ _
2. This means attractive or nice to look at.   p _ _ _ _ _
3. A person who can pick up heavy things is this.   s _ _ _ _ _
4. This word is the opposite of old.   y _ _ _ _
5. This means quite thin.   s _ _ _

3a Read the sentences about people. Write *N* (negative) or *P* (positive).

1. My sister is so lazy! .....
2. The person I spoke to on the phone was polite. .....
3. My new neighbour is very pleasant. .....
4. I met a very boring man at that party last night. .....
5. What a sweet little boy! .....
6. Your friend is really funny! .....

3b Write a few sentences about someone in your family or a friend.

....
....
....
....
....
....
....
....
....
....

⊙ Get it right!

Look at the sentence below. Then try to correct the mistake.

Thank you for inviting for a meal.

Daily life

1 Complete the gaps in the text with the correct form of the verbs in the box.

am / is	close / closes	have / has
need / needs	take / takes	walk / walks
want / wants	work / works	

Every day I wake up at 8 am, and **(1)** .... a bus into town. I eat breakfast at a café, and then **(2)** .... to my family's shop. I **(3)** .... in the shop, helping my father. He **(4)** .... the manager of the shop. We **(5)** .... lunch at about 12:30 pm and Dad **(6)** .... the shop at 5 pm. I like my job, and I know Dad **(7)** .... me, but in the future I **(8)** .... to travel, so I'm saving money to pay for that.

☑ Exam task

2 Complete the emails. Write ONE word for each space.

● ● ●   Reply   Forward

Hi Jenni,
How are you? Is your new life **(1)** .... Canada going well? **(2)** .... is your university course like? **(3)** .... you made new friends? **(4)** .... you think you might come back for a visit soon? **(5)** .... you have time, write to me.
Clara

● ● ●   Reply   Forward

Hi Clara!
I'm fine, thanks. I've **(6)** .... here for a month now. It was quite difficult for the first few weeks **(7)** .... I didn't know anyone, but now that I know more people, I'm starting **(8)** .... enjoy myself. I'm sure I **(9)** .... come home for a few weeks at the end of **(10)** .... year. I really want to see my friends and family!
Keep writing to me!
Jenni

3a Complete Jenni's next email to Clara with the correct alternatives.

Reply   Forward

Dear Clara,

You asked me (1) *that / what* I do every day. Well, I get up early (2) *because / so* my first class is (3) *at / in* 8 am. I drive to the university. (4) *After / When* I'm not in class, I usually go to the library to study and I meet friends (5) *with / for* lunch. In the evenings (6) *there / here* are concerts and sometimes parties. I go to some of (7) *they / them* with my friends, (8) *but / as* I also study a lot.

3b Imagine that a friend has asked you what you do each day. Write an email to them about your typical day.

....
....
....
....
....
....
....
....
....
....

☑ **Exam facts**

- In this part, you read two short texts. These are usually two messages.
- There are ten missing words in the texts.
- You have to write the ten missing words.

© Cambridge University Press and UCLES 2015

Social interaction

1 Complete the sentences with the correct alternatives.

1. I *would / may* see him later, but I'm not sure.
2. *May / Can* you swim a kilometre?
3. Do you think I *should / shall* invite him?
4. I *would / might* go to the party if I'm not too tired.
5. *Could / Would* you like to come to dinner tomorrow?
6. My brother *shouldn't / couldn't* walk until he was nearly two!
7. *Shall / Would* I help you get lunch ready?
8. Excuse me – you *mustn't / might not* smoke in here!

2a Complete the conversation with the correct form of the verb in brackets.

Gleb: Hi, Jan. I **(1)** .... (not / see) you for ages! What **(2)** .... (you / do) here?

Jan: I **(3)** .... (visit) my sister. She **(4)** .... (live) here for about three months.

Gleb: Oh, great! And **(5)** .... (you / still / study) at college?

Jan: Yes, but not Maths. I **(6)** .... (do) business now. What about you?

Gleb: I **(7)** .... (work) in an office at the moment, but I **(8)** .... (want) to go travelling next year.

Jan: Well, good luck with that. It was nice to see you, Gleb!

2b Write a few sentences about your plans for the weekend.

....
....
....
....
....
....
....
....
....
....

3 Complete the emails. Write ONE word for each space.

● ● ●   Reply   Forward

Hi Kris
I'm going cycling with my brother on Sunday. Would you
(1) .... to come? Don't worry if you don't (2) ....
a good bike – we've got (3) .... you can borrow. We'll
take a picnic (4) .... we won't need to eat in a café.
Let (5) .... know if you want to come.
Ali

● ● ●   Reply   Forward

Hi Ali
That's a great idea. Thanks (6) .... offering me a bike, but I got a new one a few
weeks (7) .... I'll bring lunch and something to drink. (8) .... there anything
else that I should bring? Also, (9) .... you know what time we'll be home? I need to
know (10) .... I'm going out in the evening.
Kris

☑ **Exam tips**

• Quickly read the texts before you write the missing words.

• Look at the words that come before and after the space and think about what kind of word you
  need to write – for example a noun, verb, preposition, etc.

• Only write one word in each space.

• When you finish, read the texts again to make sure they make sense.

Travel and holidays

1

Complete the text with the correct form of the verbs in brackets.

Last year I **(1)** .... (go) on holiday to France. We **(2)** .... (drive) there, which took a long time, but it **(3)** .... (be) good because we **(4)** .... (see) a lot of beautiful countryside on the way. We stayed in a lovely house which **(5)** .... (have) a really big swimming pool. Every day we **(6)** .... (get) up late and **(7)** .... (spend) all day in the sun. We **(8)** .... (eat) fantastic food too. I would like to go to the same place again next year.

 **Exam task**

2

Complete the email. Write ONE word for each space.

Reply   Forward

Hi Mum and Dad,
I hope everyone is OK at home. I arrived in New Zealand yesterday. On the plane I sat next **(1)** .... a really nice woman **(2)** .... told me about lots of places I **(3)** .... visit while I'm here. And I found a place to stay **(4)** .... isn't too expensive.
I'm going to be in New Zealand **(5)** .... a month, and then I'm going to fly to **(6)** .... USA. Dad, **(7)** .... you remember to tell **(8)** .... friend Patricia in San Francisco that I will be there next month? Has she said **(9)** .... it's okay for me to stay **(10)** .... her?
I'll write again soon.
Sonia

3 Put the words in the correct order to make questions and sentences about holiday plans.

1. year / you / are / this / where / holiday / on / going / ?

....

2. to / the / we / be / at / by / airport / ten / need / .

....

3. year / like / to / next / to / Germany / would / I / go / .

....

4. airport / are / how / the / you / to / getting / ?

....

5. to / family / I / China / going / with / am / my / .

....

6. you / long / will / how / there / stay / ?

....

7. small / a / we / hotel / to / are / stay / in / going / .

....

8. by / you / yourself / going / are / travelling / ?

....

 **Get it right!**

Look at the sentence below. Then try to correct the mistake.

Now I write a postcard to you and then I'm going to lunch at the new restaurant on the beach.

Hobbies and leisure

1 Match the sentences with the type of information they give.

1. I'll wait for you outside the cinema.
2. It starts at two thirty, so be there by two.
3. Ari's coming, so there'll be three of us.
4. With our student discount, it's six pounds.
5. We're going to see *Gate to the Forest*.
6. Let's go by bus.
7. It's on March 14th.
8. We're eating at Dan's Pizza Place.

a how to get somewhere
b number of people
c time to meet
d name of the film
e name of the restaurant
f place to meet
g price to pay
h date of event

☑ Exam task

2 Read the advertisement and the email.
Fill in the information in Jaya's notes.

Highstep Dance School
Jazz, ballet and street dance
Class dates: September 3rd to October 29th.
Classes for beginners and advanced students.
Small classes – no more than five in a group.
£5 per class or £30 for the term

●●●		
	Reply	**Forward**
From: Hannah	To: Jaya	

About our ballet dance lessons – the advanced class at Star Dance School is full! There's another school called *Highstep*. Can you call them and book for the two of us? Let's pay for the whole term – it's cheaper!

Jaya's Notes
Dance Classes
Type of dance: *ballet*
Name of school: **1** ....
Our level: **2** ....
Number of people to book for: **3** ....
Date of first class: **4** ....
Price I'll pay: **5** ....

3a 🔊 Track 4 **Listen to the conversations. Are the sentences TRUE or FALSE?**

1. The woman likes going to the beach. ....
2. The man likes his new hobby. ....
3. Dancing is the man's favourite activity. ....
4. The woman would like to go on holiday. ....
5. The woman wants to go camping. ....
6. The man likes parties. ....
7. The man wants to have a barbecue. ....
8. The woman would like the man to take a photo of her. ....

3b **Write a few sentences about hobbies you would like to try.**

....

....

....

....

....

....

....

....

....

....

....

☑ **Exam facts**

- In this part, you read two short texts.
- You have to find five pieces of information (words and numbers) in the texts.
- You use this information to complete some notes.

© Cambridge University Press and UCLES 2015

Sport and activities

1

Complete the sentences with the correct alternatives.

1. You can play football in the park, but famous teams play their matches in *playgrounds / stadiums*.
2. You might go swimming in the sea, or in *a pool / an office*.
3. At a sports *station / centre* you can do lots of different sports.
4. If you play tennis or badminton, you will need a *skate / racket*.
5. Members of a sports team wear the same colour *kit / suit* when they're playing.
6. When you play cricket or baseball, you hit the ball with a *bat / fly*.
7. In a football match, the winning team is the one that gets the most *prizes / goals*.
8. If you play a sport a lot, you might join a *club / competition*.

☑ Exam task

2

Read the advertisement and the email.
Fill in the information in Felix's notes.

Kingsfield Sports Centre – open daily from 7 am to 10 pm

NEW – tennis and badminton

Tuesday or Friday only

£7 per game (£5 for students)

Call 3464 4754 to book – payment by credit card. No cash.

● ● ●   <u>Reply</u>   <u>Forward</u>

From: Cara   To: Felix

Can you book a game for us at the sports centre? I don't have a credit card. You can play on two different days, but I'm working until 9 pm on Tuesday. Book for 7 pm, and let's play badminton – it's easier than tennis! We get a discount because we're students.

Felix's Notes
Game with Cara

Name of sports centre: *Kingsfield*

Sport we'll play: **1** ....

Day we'll play: **2** ....

Time we'll start: **3** ....

Price we'll pay: **4** ....

How we'll pay: **5** ....

3 Samuel needs to complete a form to join a sports centre. Complete the form with the correct information from the box (a–h).

a swimming and tennis	**b** by credit card	**c** sbraun@redmail.co	**d** no
e 12	**f** Mr	**g** Station Road	**h** my mother, Stella Braun

Title: (1) ....

Full name: Samuel Braun

Date of birth: 15 / 07 / 1998

Flat / House number: (2) ....

Street Name: (3) ....

Post code: 16370

Phone number: 01433 45745

Email address: (4) ....

Who should we contact if you have an accident at the sports centre? **(5)** ....

What is the contact number of this person? 01433 546 858

Are you taking any medicine at the moment? **(6)** ....

How do you want to pay? **(7)** ....

Which sports are you most interested in doing here? **(8)** ....

☑ Exam tips

- You need to read both texts to find the five answers.
- Look at the notes and think about what kind of information you have to find for each question – for example, a date, time, place, a price, etc.
- You must use words and numbers from the texts to complete the notes.
- Make sure you copy the words and numbers correctly.

Food and drink

1a Complete the table with the words from the box.

| carrot | chicken | grapes | melon | pear |
| pepper | potato | sausages | steak | |

vegetables	fruit	meat
....	....	....
....	....	....
....	....	....

1b Add more food words you know to the table. Can you think of any dishes that you could make with some of these ingredients?

 **Exam task**

2 Read the advertisement and the email.

Fill in the information in Ralf's notes.

The Orange House

Excellent Italian cooking

Open Tuesday to Saturday, 11 am to 11 pm

10% discount on Tuesdays and Wednesdays

Call 0345 48234 to book

●●●   Reply   Forward

From: Theo   To: Ralf

About Oscar's birthday - he likes French and Italian food, so let's try that restaurant in the advertisement. His birthday is on Thursday, but we'll go on Wednesday to get the discount. There'll be six of us, because two of the people I asked can't come. Book the restaurant for 8 pm, but let's meet at 7:45 pm. It closes at 11 pm.

Ralf's Notes
Restaurant for Oscar's birthday

Number to call: *0345 48234*

Type of food: **1** ....

Day to book: **2** ....

Time to book: **3** ....

Number of people: **4** ....

Time to meet: **5** ....

3a Number the instructions from a recipe for fruit salad in the correct order.

a   Add lemon juice and sugar to the large bowl with the fruit. ....

b   Serve your fruit salad ....

c   Wash the fruit. ....

d   Mix the fruit, juice and sugar together. ....

e   Choose the fruit you want to use. ....

f   Put the fruit salad into smaller bowls. ....

g   Put the fruit you have cut into a large bowl. ....

h   Cut the fruit into small pieces. ....

3b Write the instructions for a recipe you know.

....
....
....
....
....
....
....
....
....
....

Get it right!

Look at the sentences below and choose the correct one.

I get a watch and a very good necklace and many more presents.

I got a watch and a very good necklace and many more presents.

Health and exercise

1 ▸ Read the email and the reply. Complete the reply with the correct alternatives.

● ● ●   <u>Reply</u>   <u>Forward</u>

To: Richard   From: Ash

I would like to join the gym you go to. Where is it? Which activities does it offer? Can I go there with you soon?

● ● ●   <u>Reply</u>   <u>Forward</u>

Dear Ash,
The gym **(1)** *is / am* on Station Road. I usually **(2)** *taking / take* exercise classes there,
(3) *but / so* yesterday I **(4)** *use / used* the pool. There **(5)** *are / is* exercise machines too.
(6) *I'm going / I go* there tomorrow. Why **(7)** *aren't you coming / don't you come* with me?
See you soon.
Richard

2a ▸ Complete the tips about writing emails with the correct alternatives.

> When you write an email to a friend, start the email with **(1)** *Dear / Fair* or **(2)** *Hey / Hi*, and then your friend's **(3)** *title / name*.
> To finish your message you can write **(4)** *'best / good* wishes' or 'see you **(5)** *soon / quickly*.

2b ▸ Write a few sentences about your favourite kind of exercise.

....
....
....
....
....
....
....
....
....
....

3 Your English friend Jo goes running every day. You want to go running with Jo. Write an email to Jo.

- say when you want to run with Jo

- ask what time Jo goes running

- offer to show Jo a nice place to go running.

Write **25–35** words.

....

....

....

- In this part, you read a short text asking you for three pieces of information.

- The text may be a message or some notes.

- You have to write the three pieces of information in a short message.

Personal identification

1

Match the definitions with the family words.

1. your mother's brother	**a** grandmother
2. your aunt's son	**b** cousin
3. your father's mother	**c** grandchild
4. your son's daughter	**d** father
5. your sister's son	**e** nephew
6. your grandfather's son	**f** uncle

2

Complete the dialogue with the information from the boxes (a–d).

a 0648 546824.

b The fifth of October, 2000.

c Elsa Merton. That's M-E-R-T-O-N.

d 116, Greenwood Road.

Librarian: You can join the library, but I need some information first. Can you tell me your full name, please?

Elsa: (1) ....

Librarian: Thank you. And where do you live, Elsa?

Elsa: (2) ....

Librarian: That's fine. Now – what's your date of birth?

Elsa: (3) ....

Librarian: OK. And finally, what's your phone number?

Elsa: (4) ....

Librarian: Thank you Elsa. Here's your card and your book. Now I'll show you around the library.

3 Read the email from your English friend, Maxi.

		Reply	Forward

●●●

To: From: Maxi

I've received a wedding invitation from your brother. It's so nice of him! Can you suggest a place in your city where I can stay? What do people usually wear to weddings in your country? What can I buy them for a present?

Write an email to Maxi and answer the questions.

Write 25–35 words.

....
....
....
....
....
....
....
....
....
....

- Read the instructions carefully to find out what you need to write.
- You must write all three pieces of information.
- When you finish your message, check your spelling and grammar.

Entertainment and media

1 Complete the sentences with the words in the box.

actor	channel	exhibition	fan
movie	screen	stage	video games

1. If you don't like the TV programme, change the ....
2. My friend is a big .... of that group. She goes to all their concerts.
3. I love playing .... online with my friends.
4. I'm going to that photography .... at the museum tomorrow.
5. Let's see that film. Your favourite .... is in it.
6. The .... at that new cinema is really big.
7. I didn't have a good seat at the theatre. I was a long way from the ....
8. Another word for a film is a ....

2 Add the punctuation (question marks, full stops, capital letters and apostrophes) to the sentences.

1. Id like to go to that concert

....

2. are you going to the party tonight

....

3. my friend sara is going to be in a show

....

4. this isnt carlas guitar

....

5. ive never been to the opera

....

6. i dont like that artist

....

7. i think well need to buy a ticket

....

8. do you know where i live

....

3

Your English friend Charlie has invited you to the cinema tomorrow, but you can't go.

Write an email to Charlie.

- tell Charlie that you are sorry
- explain why you can't go
- say which day you can go instead.

Write **25–35** words.

....

....

....

Get it right!

Look at the sentence below. Then try to correct the mistake.

I'm having a day off next week I would like to come to visit you.

KEY LISTENING PART 1

Services and places

1 Match the question to the answer.

1. When shall we meet?	**a** At 8:30 am every day.
2. What time does the next train leave?	**b** At 6:15 pm, outside the cinema.
3. When is your sister's birthday?	**c** At twenty to eight, on platform three.
4. What time does the post office open?	**d** In 2009. We were in the same class at school.
5. When is your doctor's appointment?	**e** Saturday. I love the weekend!
6. How long have you lived in Sydney?	**f** Next Wednesday at 1:15 pm.
7. When do you play hockey?	**g** On the 22nd September.
8. Excuse me, what's the time please?	**h** On Tuesdays, in the sports centre.
9. When did you meet your best friend?	**i** Since 2014.
10. What's your favourite day of the week?	**j** It's ten o'clock.

☑ Exam task

2 🔊 Track 5 You will hear five short conversations.
You will hear each conversation twice.
There is one question for each conversation.
For questions 1–5, put a tick (✓) under the right answer.

1. Where is the post office?

 A ☐  B ☐  C ☐

2. What does the man order?

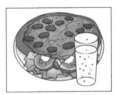 A ☐ 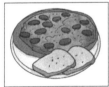 B ☐ 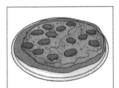 C ☐

3. How much does the man spend?

 A ☐  B ☐  C ☐

4. Where are the girls going today?

A ☐

B ☐

C ☐

5. When is the woman going to the dentist?

A ☐

B ☐

C ☐

3 Match the words in the box to the sentences and questions.

cinema	dentist	hotel	library	museum	restaurant
sports centre	theatre		tourist information centre		train station

1. The paintings were discovered in Italy in 1843. ....

2. Excuse me, what time does the play finish? ....

3. Can I have a return ticket to Bradford, please? ....

4. You are in room 321, on the third floor. Here is the key. Enjoy your stay. ....

5. I'll have a chicken salad, please. ....

6. Would you like a map of the city? ....

7. Good morning. I've got an appointment at 4:30. ....

8. What time does the aerobics class start? ....

9. Let's buy tickets for the new James Bond film now! ....

10. Can I borrow these books, please? ....

☑ *Exam facts*

- In this part, you listen to five short conversations.
- There are five questions with three pictures.
- You have to choose the right picture.

Shopping and numbers

1 Complete the sentences with the numbers in the box.

| eight | fifteen | seven | sixty | twelve | twenty-six | two hundred | thousand |

1. There are .... days in a week.
2. When it's 11:45, it is also a quarter to ....
3. There are a .... metres in a kilometre.
4. I'm 24 and my sister is 16. She's .... years younger than me.
5. There are .... seconds in a minute.
6. Paula lives at 16 Brick Lane and her friend lives next door at number ....
7. There are .... letters in the English alphabet.
8. Our house was built in 1793. It's over .... years old.

☑ Exam task

2 🔊 Track 6 You will hear five short conversations.
You will hear each conversation twice.
There is one question for each conversation.
For questions 1–5, put a tick (✓) under the right answer.

1. Which bus goes to the supermarket?

 A ☐

 B ☐

 C ☐

2. What time does the shop close?

 A ☐

 B ☐

 C ☐

3. Which T-shirt does the woman buy?

 A ☐

 B ☐

 C ☐

4. What time does the bookshop close on Saturday?

 A ☐  B ☐  C ☐

5. What did the man buy?

 A ☐  B ☐  C ☐

3 ▶ **Read the descriptions and complete the words. The first letter is given to you. There is one space for each letter in the word.**

1. If you haven't got any cash you will need to pay with this. c _ _ _ _ _   c _ _ _

2. When you buy something the shop assistant will give you this. r _ _ _ _ _ _

3. This is a shop with many floors where you can buy lots of different things. d _ _ _ _ _ _ _ _ _
   s _ _ _ _

4. These are people who buy things in a shop. c _ _ _ _ _ _ _ _

5. There are 100 pennies in one of these. p _ _ _ _

6. You can buy food and other things in this shop. s _ _ _ _ _ _ _ _ _

7. You might do this before you buy new clothes. t _ _ (them) _ _

8. If you like reading, you might go to this shop. b _ _ _ _ _ _ _

9. Shoppers in America spend these. d _ _ _ _ _ _

10. When you are shopping you can ask this person for help. a _ _ _ _ _ _ _ _

✓ **Exam tips**

• Read the questions very carefully. <u>Underline</u> the most important words in the question.

• The people will talk about what you can see in all three pictures, but only one is right.

• The first time you listen, choose your answers. The second time you listen, check that your answers are right.

Education and study

1 Choose the correct alternative.

1. What time *did / does* the class finish last week?
2. Fran is always tired on Saturdays so she *got up / gets up* late.
3. *Was / Does* your mum work in a bank?
4. Max *bought / is going to buy* a new mobile phone later.
5. Kate *sends / sent* me an email two days ago.
6. *Did you / Are you going to* visit your grandmother tomorrow?
7. I sometimes *meet / am going to meet* my friends at the beach.
8. *Is / Was* Ben wearing a hat at the party last night?
9. I think *I'll go / I went* shopping tomorrow.
10. Matt usually walks home but this afternoon he is going to *ride / rides* his bike.

☑ Exam task

2 Track 7

You will hear five short conversations.
You will hear each conversation twice.
There is one question for each conversation.
For questions 1–5, put a tick (✓) under the right answer.

1. What is the boy's favourite subject?

A ☐

B ☐

C ☐

2. Where does the girl put the dictionary?

A ☐

B ☐

C ☐

3. What does the boy lend the girl?

A ☐

B ☐

C ☐

4. What time does the TV programme start?

 A ☐  B ☐  C ☐

5. Where does the boy have lessons?

 A ☐  B ☐  C ☐

3 ▶ **Read about Teresa's day, then choose the correct alternative.**

Hello. My name's Teresa. I am a teacher in a Secondary School. I usually wake up at 7:30, I have a shower and get dressed. Then I have toast for breakfast. I always listen to the news on the radio while I am having breakfast. I leave the house at 8:30 and I cycle to work. I start at 9:00 and school finishes at 4:15. After work, I often go to the pool. When I get home, I make dinner, and eat it in the living room while I watch TV. After dinner I do the washing up, walk my dog on the beach and sometimes phone my friends. I usually go to bed at 10:30. I love reading travel magazines and always look at them before I go to sleep.

1. Teresa works in a *bank / school*.

2. She has *cereal / toast* for breakfast.

3. While she is having breakfast, she listens to *music / the news*.

4. Teresa goes to work by *bike / car*.

5. She starts work at *eight thirty / nine o'clock*.

6. After work, she often *shops / swims*.

7. She watches TV while she is *cooking / eating*.

8. She eats dinner in the *living room / kitchen*.

9. She walks her dog *in the park / on the beach*.

10. She usually reads *emails / magazines* before she goes to sleep.

 **Get it right!**

Look at the sentences below and choose the correct one.

Next week I'm going to an interesting place near your town.

Next week, I go to an interesting place near your town.

Food and drink

1 Look at the picture and complete the questions with the words in the box. Then write the questions.

that	these	this	those

1. What's .... ? It's milk.
2. What's .... ? It's a cake.
3. What are .... ? They're crisps.
4. What are .... ? They're biscuits.

5. .... ? They're sandwiches.
6. .... ? It's cola.
7. .... ? They're strawberries.
8. .... ? It's water.

☑ Exam task

2 🔊 Track 8
Listen to Sarah and Mike talking about food and drink for a picnic.
What is each person going to take to the picnic?
For questions 1–5, write the letter A–H next to each person.
You will hear the conversation twice.

People

1 Mike ☐
2 Margaret ☐
3 John ☐
4 Andrea ☐
5 Eric ☐

Food and drink

A apples
B biscuits
C cakes
D cola
E hamburgers
F ice cream
G sandwiches
H strawberries

3a Write *C* (countable) or *UC* (uncountable) next to each word.

1. biscuit _ _	**5.** egg _ _	**9.** milk _ _	**13.** sandwich _ _
2. bread _ _	**6.** grape _ _	**10.** orange _ _	**14.** sausage _ _
3. crisp _ _	**7.** hamburger _ _	**11.** pasta _ _	**15.** sugar _ _
4. cheese _ _	**8.** meat _ _	**12.** salad _ _	**16.** water _ _

3b Choose the correct alternative.

1. There isn't much *hamburgers / cheese* in the fridge.

2. There aren't many *oranges / milk* in the supermarket.

3. There are a lot of *biscuits / sugar* in our shopping basket.

4. There is a lot of *sausages / pasta* on my plate!

5. There are a few *apples / sugar* in the cupboard.

6. There is a little *eggs / bread* on the table.

7. There *is / are* a lot of salad in this sandwich!

8. There isn't *many / much* water in the bottle.

9. There are a *few / little* grapes in the bowl.

10. *Are / Is* there any crisps in the bag?

11. There aren't *many / much* sandwiches in the shop.

12. There is a *few / little* meat in the freezer.

☑ **Exam facts**

- In this part, you listen to a conversation between two people who know each other.
- You have to match two lists of information.

Hobbies and shopping

1 Look at the table and read the sentences. Are they TRUE or FALSE?

	Surfing	Playing computer games	Going shopping	Dancing
Agatha	✓✓	✗	✓	✗
Hugh	✓✓✓	✓	✗	✓
Vanessa	✓	✓✓	✗	✓✓✓

1. Agatha likes playing computer games. ....
2. Hugh thinks surfing is more interesting than dancing. ....
3. Vanessa prefers surfing to dancing. ....
4. Agatha enjoys surfing and dancing. ....
5. Hugh's favourite hobby is playing computer games. ....
6. Vanessa is not interested in going shopping. ....
7. Agatha doesn't like playing computer games or dancing. ....
8. Hugh thinks playing computer games is boring. ....
9. Agatha prefers going shopping to dancing. ....
10. Hugh and Vanessa don't enjoy going shopping. ....

☑ Exam task

2 🔊 Track 9

Listen to Sonia and Dan talking about shopping.
What did Sonia buy in each shop?
For questions 1–5, write the letter A–H next to each shop.
You will hear the conversation twice.

Shops

1 clothes shop ☐
2 bookshop ☐
3 supermarket ☐
4 sports shop ☐
5 market ☐

Things

A bag
B cake
C flowers
D shampoo
E socks
F towel
G trainers
H trousers

Choose the correct response to each question, a, b or c.

1. Can I help you?
   a Yes, please.   **b** Pleased to meet you.   **c** Good bye.

2. Could I try this on, please?
   a It's £10.   **b** Yes, of course.   **c** It's very big.

3. Would you like me to put the receipt in the bag?
   a No, thanks.   **b** That's nice.   **c** It's very heavy.

4. Should I make dinner this evening?
   a No, it's OK. I'll do it.   **b** I don't like it.   **c** I'll have a ham and cheese pizza, please.

5. Can I take your order?
   a A table for two, please.   **b** OK, thank you.   **c** Yes. Two hamburgers, please.

6. Would you carry this bag for me, please?
   a Yes, please.   **b** Yes, of course.   **c** No, I wouldn't.

7. Can I have two return tickets to Manchester, please?
   a When do you want to travel?   **b** That's fine.   **c** How much is it?

8. Shall I go to the supermarket this afternoon?
   a Yes, I like chicken.   **b** No, we will have chicken for dinner.   **c** Yes, can you buy some chicken?

9. Could you close the window, please?
   a Yes, are you cold?   **b** No, I'm cold.   **c** Yes, I'm sorry.

10. Would you like a drink?
    a No, I'm not hungry.   **b** No, thanks.   **c** Yes, an ice cream please.

Write four sentences about yourself. Use _enjoy / favourite / prefer ... to / don't like._

1. ....
2. ....
3. ....
4. ....

☑ Exam tips

- Before you listen, read the two lists and think about what the conversation might be about.
- In the second list, the words you hear are often different from the words you read.
- You can only use an answer once. When you have used an answer, ~~cross it out~~.

Countries and sports

1 Complete the table with the correct words.

Country	Nationality	Language
(1)	Australian	English
Brazil	(2)	Portuguese
The United Kingdom	British	(3) ....
(4)	Chinese	Chinese
France	(5)	French
(6)	Mexican	Spanish
Italy	Italian	(7) ....
Turkey	(8)	Turkish

☑ *Exam task*

2 🔊 Track 10

Listen to Tanya talk to a friend about a sports camp.
Which sport did each person try?
For questions 1–5, write the letter A–H next to each person.
You will hear the conversation twice.

People

1 Chris ☐
2 Gina ☐
3 Tom ☐
4 Emma ☐
5 Harry ☐

Sports

A basketball

B climbing

C golf

D horse riding

E sailing

F swimming

G tennis

H windsurfing

3 Put the words in the correct order to make suggestions. Use the responses to help you.

1. don't / Why / we / on / shopping / go / Thursday / ?

....

No, I don't like shopping!

2. go / you / like / to / at / skiing / the / Would / weekend / ?

....

I'd love to, but I have to work.

3. beach / running / morning / on / the / Let's / to / tomorrow / go /.

....

Good idea!

4. want / to / Do / play / you / at / tennis / after / school / ?

....

No, sorry. I can't.

5. a / we / movie / Shall / watch / later / ?

....

OK. We can see the new Tom Cruise film.

6. walk / going / What / for / a / park / in / afternoon / about / the / this / ?

....

No, that's boring, but we could go skateboarding instead!

 Get it right!

Look at the sentences below. Then try to correct the mistake in each one.

I like listening to musics and seeing films.
Did you get much presents?

Leisure time

1 Match the questions and answers. Then underline the answer word(s).

1. How much did you pay for that video game, Chris? ....
2. Was it sunny in France last week, Jane? ....
3. When do you have dance lessons, Alex? ....
4. What time does the picnic start on Sunday? ....
5. When are you going to the *One Star* concert in London? ....
6. Where did Bella learn English? ....

a   They are playing for three nights, but my ticket's for the 25th September.

b   The full price is £15, but my brother works in the computer shop and he gets a discount, so I only paid £12!

c   At about 12.00, but I'm meeting Felix at the station at 11:30 and we're going together.

d   No, it wasn't. It was cloudy, but it didn't rain!

e   Every Friday. Do you want to come next week?

f   She lived in London for two years when she was twenty.

☑ Exam task

2 🔊 Track 11 Listen to Jack talking to his friend Martin about music.

For each question, choose the right answer (A, B or C). You will hear the conversation twice.

1 What is the name of Martin's music teacher?

  A Harry

  B Peter

  C Steve

2 Martin has music lessons on

  A Tuesdays.

  B Thursdays.

  C Saturdays.

3 How long does Martin practise at the weekend?

  A 1 hour

  B 2 hours

  C 3 hours

4 Where is the music festival?

  A at the music school

  B in the park

  C in the shopping centre

5 Martin will start playing

  A at 6:15.

  B at 7:00.

  C at 7:45.

3a Complete the table with the words in the box.

the beach	a bike	a camera	the cinema	cooking
a fishing rod	go to a festival	go to a restaurant		have a barbecue
have a picnic	a mobile phone	a museum		painting
the park	reading	taking photos		

Favourite things	Hobbies	Places to go	Things to do at the weekend
....	....	....	....
....	....	....	....
....	....	....	....
....	....	....	....

3b Answer the questions about yourself.

1. What do you do in your free time?

....

2. Can you play an instrument?

....

3. What is your favourite thing?

....

4. Where do you usually meet your friends?

....

5. How often do you go the cinema?

....

6. What did you do yesterday afternoon?

....

7. What are you going to do at the weekend?

....

8. Have you ever been to a music festival?

....

 Exam facts

- In this part, you listen to a conversation between two people.
- There are five questions and you have to choose the right answer (A, B or C).

Social media and technology

1 Put the letters in the right order to make words. Then complete the sentences.

1. I usually .... games onto my laptop computer to practise my English. (dwondaol)

2. I use my .... to call my friends, take photos and send messages. (emboil npohe)

3. You can find out about lots of things on the .... (ietrentn)

4. I often play .... in my spare time. (voied gsmae)

5. My favourite band have got an amazing .... with interesting facts and information on it. (wbe pega)

6. My sister loves taking photos with her .... (dtiliga cmraea)

7. Some people spend many hours chatting to friends .... (oinnel)

8. Q is the first letter on most .... (ekybardos)

9. You can use a .... to open and close documents on your computer. (mesuo)

10. I send lots of .... every day at work. (ealims)

✓ Exam task

2 🔊 Track 12 **Listen to Lisa talking to her friend Robert about computers.**

For each question, choose the right answer (A, B or C). You will hear the conversation twice.

1 Where did Lisa buy her laptop?

  A Bridge Street

  B Green Street

  C High Street

2 The most useful website was

  A buy_a_computer.com

  B computers_and_phones.com

  C new_laptop.com

3 Lisa's new laptop weighs

  A one kilogramme.

  B 1.5 kilogrammes.

  C two kilogrammes.

4 How much did Lisa pay for her laptop?

  A £579

  B £699

  C £849

5 Why did Lisa buy a new laptop?

  A to talk to her brother

  B to shop online

  C to study

3 **Rewrite the sentences in the past or present passive.**

1. Martin Cooper invented the first mobile phone in 1973.

....

2. Lots of people watch videos on the internet.

....

3. My brother didn't write that email.

....

4. People often read news articles online.

....

5. Tim Berners-Lee created the first website in 1991.

....

6. Young people usually play video games at home.

....

7. The teacher showed the students some useful websites.

....

 *Exam tips*

- You have to answer a question or complete a sentence.
- You will hear all three answers, but only one is right.
- The same person usually gives all of the answers.

Travel and holidays

1 Complete the sentences with the words in the box. There are some words that you do not need to use.

article	bill	comics	diary	diploma
form	magazines	menu	newspaper	passport
postcard	project	text book	ticket	

1. My little brother loves reading ....

2. We haven't finished all the exercises in our English .... yet.

3. Great! The .... in this restaurant is in English!

4. Lots of people read fashion ....

5. I usually read the .... on the train in the morning.

6. My sister writes in her .... every day.

7. Sandra, you need to get a new .... to travel to New Zealand.

8. I always send my parents a .... when I am on holiday.

9. You must keep your .... for the return journey.

10. I read an interesting .... about sport on the internet.

☑ **Exam task**

2 🔊 Track 13 **Listen to James talking to Susan about his holiday.**

For each question, choose the right answer (A, B or C).
You will hear the conversation twice.

1 How long is James's holiday?

  A one week

  B two weeks

  C three weeks

2 Where is James flying to first?

  A Manchester

  B Miami

  C Paris

3 Where did James go in January?

  A Canada

  B Mexico

  C The USA

4 How long is the flight to Miami?

  A five hours

  B 8.5 hours

  C 16 hours

5 The aeroplane arrives in Manchester at

  A 1:00 pm

  B 5:35 pm

  C 11:05 am

3a Match 1–10 with a–j.

1.	I'm	**a**	'm flying to Mallorca tomorrow.
2.	Emily and Vicky	**b**	they're going to visit the Old Town tomorrow.
3.	We're going	**c**	are travelling around the USA this summer.
4.	I'm not going to stay	**d**	coming to visit us in July.
5.	Tom	**e**	to go swimming tomorrow.
6.	My grandmother's	**f**	going to take a photo of the beach now.
7.	I	**g**	's going to take us to the lake after lunch.
8.	My brother isn't driving	**h**	lunch at half past one.
9.	We're having	**i**	on a campsite this year.
10.	My parents love sightseeing so	**j**	to France in August, he's flying.

3b Write a few sentences about your next holiday.

....

....

....

....

....

....

....

....

....

....

 **Get it right!**

Look at the sentence below. Then try to correct the mistake.

This present gave to me by my old German friend.

Making plans

1a Complete the sentences with the words in the box.

| autumn | birthday | century | clock | diary | evening | weekly | yesterday |

1. Today is Wednesday so .... was Tuesday.
2. The big .... on the wall in my office says it's 5:15 pm.
3. If you have a meeting every Monday, it's a .... meeting.
4. There are one hundred years in a ....
5. The book where people write their appointments is called a ....
6. .... is the season when the leaves fall from the trees.
7. People usually give you presents on your ....
8. The time between the afternoon and the night is called the ....

1b Complete the table with the words and phrases in the box.

every day	Friday morning	half past three	January	last year
Mondays	the afternoon	the moment	the weekend	
tomorrow	2013	15th May		

at	in	on	no preposition
....	....	....	....
....	....	....	....
....	....	....	....

☑ Exam task

2 ◀)) Track 14 You will hear a woman talking to a customer about renting a boat.

Listen and complete each question.
You will hear the conversation twice.

Customer information

Name: Philip Cook

Birthday: 1st December **(1)** ....

Number of people to rent boat: **(2)** ....

Pets: **(3)** ....

Dates: From 23rd August – **(4)** ....

Phone number: **(5)** ....

Read the dialogue. Choose the best word for each space, a, b or c.

Mario: Hello Tanya. Where are you **(1)** .... to go on holiday this year?

Tanya: I **(2)** .... going to go to Tenerife in August.

Mario: That sounds fun! Will it be hot?

Tanya: Yes, it **(3)** ..... I've bought a new hat and some sunglasses.

Mario: Really? Who **(4)** .... you going to go with?

Tanya: With my friends Lara and Michelle.

Mario: My sister went to Tenerife last year. She said that the beaches are amazing.

Tanya: I know. But we **(5)** .... have a lot of free time to explore the island!

Mario: Why not? What are you going to do?

Tanya: We **(6)** .... going to study Spanish in a language school.

Mario: That sounds fun. Are you going **(7)** .... lessons every day?

Tanya: Yes, we are.

Mario: Do you think you **(8)** .... be in the same class as your friends?

Tanya: No, we **(9)** .... be, because my friends speak better Spanish than me.

Mario: **(10)** .... you send me a postcard?

Tanya: Yes, of course! What's your address?

1.	**a** going	**b** doing	**c** will
2.	**a** 'm	**b** 's	**c** 'll
3.	**a** going	**b** is	**c** will
4.	**a** is	**b** are	**c** will
5.	**a** am	**b** will	**c** won't
6.	**a** 'm	**b** 're	**c** 'll
7.	**a** has	**b** have	**c** to have
8.	**a** are	**b** will	**c** is
9.	**a** aren't	**b** will	**c** won't
10.	**a** will	**b** going to	**c** are

☑ **Exam facts**

- In this part, you listen to a short conversation between two people.
- There is a form that you have to complete with words and numbers.

© Cambridge University Press and UCLES 2015

Health, medicine and exercise

1 Read the descriptions and complete the words. The first letter is given to you. There is one space for each letter in the word.

1. Some animals have got a big one of these, for example humans and dolphins. b _ _ _ _

2. If you have a problem with this, you go to the dentist. t _ _ _ _

3. You use these to see. e _ _ _

4. This might be curly or straight. h _ _ _

5. You wear shoes on these. f _ _ _

6. This is between your head and your body. n _ _ _

7. You have ten of these on your hands. f _ _ _ _ _ _

8. This moves your blood around your body. h _ _ _ _

9. If you eat a lot of cake, you might have a pain here. s _ _ _ _ _ _

10. Some people write with their left one of these. h _ _ _

☑ *Exam task*

2 🔊 Track 15 You will hear a man telephoning a medical centre for advice.

Listen and complete each question.
You will hear the conversation twice.

Medical advice

Address of chemist: Park Street

Cost of taxi: € **(1)** ....

Doctor's name: Doctor **(2)** ....

Time of appointment: **(3)** ....

Doctor speaks: **(4)** ....

Hospital phone number: **(5)** ....

3 Read the conversations. Choose the correct modal verb.

1. I've got a toothache.

   You *might / should* go to the dentist!

2. Chris has fallen off his motorbike and now his arm hurts.

   It *might / should* be broken so he *might not / shouldn't* move.

3. Emma fell over when she was running and has hurt her ankle.

   I think she *might / should* put a bandage on it.

4. I've got a headache.

   You *might / should* lie down in your bedroom and take this medicine.

5. Can you help me? I've cut my hand on a rock.

   There is a lot of blood so you *might / should* see a doctor.

6. Lucy is very hot.

   She *might not / shouldn't* go to school today because she *might / should* have a temperature.

7. I'm really tired and I don't feel well.

   You *might / should* go to bed, you will feel better tomorrow.

8. Mum, I feel sick. My stomach hurts.

   You *might not / shouldn't* eat any more sweets, Jeremy. And take some medicine.

☑ Exam tips

- Before you listen, read the form carefully.
- Think about what kind of information you need to write for each question – for example, a day, time, name, phone number, etc.
- You usually have to write the name of a person or place. One of the speakers will spell it.

Dates and services

1a Match the numbers to the words.

1st	fifth
2nd	first
3rd	fourteenth
4th	fourth
5th	ninth
9th	second
12th	third
13th	thirteenth
14th	thirty-first
20th	twelfth
25th	twentieth
31st	twenty-fifth

1b Complete the sentences with the words from Exercise 1a.

1. The listening paper is the .... part of the exam.
2. March is the .... month of the year.
3. *E* is the .... letter of the alphabet.
4. December is the .... month of the year.
5. Halloween is on the .... of October.
6. *M* is the .... letter of the alphabet.
7. Christmas Day is on the .... of December.
8. September is the .... month of the year.
9. Valentine's Day is on the .... of February.
10. April is the .... month of the year.
11. *T* is the .... letter of the alphabet.
12. New Year's Day is on the .... of January.

 **Get it right!**

Look at the sentences below and choose the correct one.

It is very important to me because I will go to New Zealand tomorrow.

It is very important to me because I am going to New Zealand tomorrow.

☑ *Exam task*

🔊 **Track 16 You will hear a woman talking to a receptionist about photography lessons.**

Listen and complete each question.
You will hear the conversation twice.

Photography lessons

Start: 3rd October
Classes on: **(1)** ....
Evening course costs: **(2)** £ ....
College closed in: **(3)** ....
Opening hours: Monday to Friday 9:30 am to 12:45 pm and 5:30 pm to **(4)** ....
Address: **(5)** 59 ....

Choose the correct response to each question, a, b or c.

1. What time does the museum close at the weekend?
   a It opens on Saturdays. **b** At half past seven.　　　**c** Yes, every week.

2. When is your birthday?
   a It's at five o'clock.　　**b** It's in 1995.　　　**c** It's on the 3rd May.

3. When is your favourite programme on TV?
   a On the 6th December. **b** On Wednesday evenings.　**c** I saw it last September.

4. Do you have swimming lessons on Tuesdays?
   a No, last week.　　　**b** On Mondays.　　　**c** Yes, from seven to eight in the evening.

5. When are you going on holiday?
   a On the 13th October.　**b** Yesterday, with my parents. **c** On Tuesdays from 7 pm – 9 pm.

6. What time do you get up?
   a In the morning.　　　**b** At a quarter past seven on　**c** It's nine o'clock in the morning.
   　　　　　　　　　　　　　weekdays.

7. When will the new video game be on sale?
   a I play it every week.　**b** Last week. It was great.　**c** In the spring, I think.

8. Is the sports centre open on Sundays?
   a Yes, it opens at 9 am. **b** It's open every day from　**c** No, it closes at 5 pm.
   　　　　　　　　　　　　　Monday to Saturday.

House and home

1 Read the sentences. Choose the correct word for each space, a, b or c.

1. Can you tell me your .... please?

    a address   **b** apartment   **c** house

2. Many British houses have got .... on the floor.

    a carpet   **b** curtains   **c** downstairs

3. I haven't got a .... so I have to park my car on the street.

    a gate   **b** garage   **c** roof

4. Some people sing when they are in the .... .

    a cupboard   **b** sink   **c** shower

5. It was cold last night so I got an extra .... from the cupboard.

    a blanket   **b** pillow   **c** lamp

6. Oh no! I've lost my house .... . Can you lend me yours, please?

    a doors   **b** computers   **c** keys

7. My brother lives in a flat on the third .... of a building.

    a door   **b** floor   **c** room

8. I need to go shopping because there isn't any milk in the .... .

    a book shelves   **b** cooker   **c** fridge

9. There's a comfortable .... in my living room.

    a armchair   **b** bed   **c** television

10. Can you put a clean .... in the bathroom, please?

    a clock   **b** desk   **c** towel

☑ Exam task

2 🔊 Track 17 **You will hear a radio programme about a house.**

**Listen and complete each question.
You will hear the information twice.**

Matt Jackson's house

Age: 100 years old

Number of floors **(1)** ....

Hall: Photos of children and **(2)** ....

Living room: Long, green **(3)** ....

An old wooden **(4)** ....

Garden: colourful flowers and **(5)** .... trees

3 Put the words into the correct order to make questions. Then write answers about where you live.

1. Do / live / you / house / a / or / in / flat / a / ?

....

2. it / How / got / bedrooms / many / has / ?

....

3. What / door / is / your / colour / front / ?

....

4. you / a / Have / garden / got / ?

....

5. TV / you / usually / do / Where / watch / ?

....

6. you / in / got / bedroom / an / Have / armchair / your / ?

....

7. Is / in / there / a / living / your / room / clock / ?

....

8. you / Do / city / in / live / a / ?

....

☑ **Exam facts**

- In this part, you listen to one person talking.
- There is a form that you have to complete with words and numbers.

© Cambridge University Press and UCLES 2015

Entertainment and the media

1a

◀)) **Track 18 Listen and write the phone numbers.**

1. _ _ _ _ _ _ _
2. _ _ _ _ _ _
3. _ _ _ _ _ _ _ _
4. _ _ _ _ _ _
5. _ _ _ _ _ _

1b

Read the information and write the correct phone numbers in words.

Emily's Language School: 4921358
Jack's Cars: 8941912
Medical Centre: 4769335
Sharps Hairdresser: 7239853
Mayfair Theatre: 6746829

1. Hello Martin, What's the phone number for the hairdresser?

It's ....

2. Can you call a taxi, please? The number is ....

3. Christina, have you got the telephone number for the English teacher?

Yes, it's ....

4. I feel sick and I think I've got a temperature.

You should call Doctor Brown on ....

5. What time does the concert finish on Saturday?

Why don't you call the ticket office and ask them? The number is ....

☑ **Exam tips**

- You will often hear two pieces of information for the same question – for example, two days, two prices, two times, etc. Listen carefully and write the right one.
- You often have to write a day of the week. Make sure you know how to spell them correctly.
- Write numbers as numbers, and not words.
- In phone numbers, for 0 we usually say 'oh'.

☑ Exam task

2 🔊 Track 19 You will hear a woman talking about a music festival.

Listen and complete each question.
You will hear the information twice.

<u>City music day</u>

Starts: 10:30 am

All day:

Activities for children aged 6– **(1)** ....

Morning: Singing competition in **(2)** ....

First prize: A ticket for *Summer Stars* festival in **(3)** ....

Afternoon: Guitar concert

Buy tickets **(4)** ....

For more information call Jackie Webb on: **(5)** ....

3 <u>Underline</u> the imperatives in the sentences. Then match the people (a–j) to the sentences (1–10).

1. Call us now to make an appointment.	**a** a football club
2. Phone Peter on 553442 about the next match.	**b** a hairdresser
3. Look on our webpage for details about the cruise.	**c** a parent
4. Shhh. Don't talk!	**d** a hotel receptionist
5. OK, everyone, show me your homework please.	**e** a teacher
6. Send me a postcard when you're on holiday!	**f** a travel agents
7. Please fill in this form before we give you your key.	**g** a tourist information office
8. Ask your partner some questions about the book club.	**h** a Cambridge English Speaking examiner
9. Paul, go to bed now!	**i** student in a library
10. Meet the tour guide outside the museum at 9 am.	**j** your friend

Education and study

1 Complete the swimming pool rules with the words in the box.

POOL RULES

don't	have (x2)	must (x2)	mustn't	not	to

1. You .... follow these rules.
2. You .... run.
3. You .... have a shower before you get into the pools.
4. You must .... eat or drink in the pools.
5. If you can't swim, you .... to stay in the small pool.
6. If you have short hair, you .... have to wear a swimming hat.
7. Children under 5 years old don't .... to pay.
8. Children under 8 years old have .... be with an adult.

☑ Exam task

2 ◀)) Track 20 You will hear a teacher talking about a school trip.

Listen and complete each question.
You will hear the information twice.

Trip to art gallery

Important information:

Wear: comfortable shoes

Arrive at school: **(1)** .... in the morning.

If you arrive late, telephone: **(2)** ....

Homework: Write about favourite: **(3)** ....

Mustn't use: Cameras or **(4)** ....

Eat lunch: **(5)** ....

3a Put the words into the correct order to make sentences.

1. You / lots / vegetables / to / of / and / eat / fruit / have / .

....

2. mustn't / in / run / corridors / You / the / !

....

3. for / You / to / take / need / this / ten / medicine / days / .

....

4. have / You / me / don't / to / help / .

....

5. your / turn / You / mobile / an / phone / in / exam / off / must / .

....

6. shout / needn't / I / You / hear / can / you / !

....

3b Read the sentences and choose the correct alternative.

1. Tom *has / must* to wear a suit to work every day.
2. We *don't have to / mustn't* touch the animals, they are dangerous!
3. Alice *must / need* speak English in the classroom!
4. Dad, you *have to / needn't* take me to the cinema, I can get the bus.
5. Jackie *doesn't have / mustn't* to go to school on Saturday mornings.
6. You *don't have / need* to call your sister this evening, she's worried about you!

◎ Get it right!

Look at the sentences below and choose the correct one.

You must to bring a book and a pencil case.
You have to bring a book and a pencil case.

Personal identification

1   Complete the conversation with the correct phrases.

Ben: Hello. My name's Ben. I've just moved to Newville.

Oliver: (1) ....

Ben: Hi, Oliver. Do you live in Newville?

Oliver: (2) ....

Ben: Oh, really! How often do you play sport there?

Oliver: (3) ....

Ben: What do you do at the weekend?

Oliver: (4) ....

Ben: Is there a shopping centre in Newville?

Oliver: (5) ....

Ben: And what's your favourite place in Newville?

Oliver: (6) ....

a   Football and tennis but I'm not very good.

b   I never shop there because I prefer to buy things online.

c   I usually meet my friends to skateboard.

d   Not very often. I like watching it on TV!

e   Pleased to meet you. I'm Oliver.

f   This park, because it's very beautiful.

g   Yes, my sister goes there every Saturday.

h   Yes, near the sports centre.

☑ Exam task

2   Put the words in the correct order to make questions or sentences. Ask and answer with a partner.

1. your / What's / name ?
2. surname / your / what's / And ?
3. spell / you / do / that / How ?
4. you / are / Where / from ?
5. English / your / Who / teacher / is ?
6. learning / start / English / When / you / did ?
7. get / up / time / the / you / morning / What / do / in ?
8. any / or / got / brothers / you / Have / sisters ?
9. you / to / often / do / How / music / listen ?
10. reading / like / Do / books / you ?
11. about / best / something / me / friend / Tell / your .
12. something / programme / favourite / Tell / your / me / TV / about .

3 Complete the sentences with the correct word. The first letter of each word is given to help you.

1. Bob is your first name, and Brown is your s _ _ _ _ _ _ .
2. You are a man. You are married. You have a w _ _ _ .
3. Eric has got a sister but he hasn't got any b _ _ _ _ _ _ _ .
4. Your mum has got a sister. She's your a _ _ _ .
5. My father's father is my g _ _ _ _ _ _ _ _ _ _ .
6. You've got a child. She's a girl. She's your d _ _ _ _ _ _ _ .
7. I am 15 years old and my brother is 17. We're both t _ _ _ _ _ _ _ _ .
8. Your uncle's got two children. They're your c _ _ _ _ _ _ .
9. The people who live near you are your n _ _ _ _ _ _ _ _ _ .
10. Your mum and dad are your p _ _ _ _ _ _ .

☑ **Exam facts**

- In this part, the examiner asks you questions about yourself.
- The questions are usually about your name, where you come from, your hobbies, where you study or work, etc.
- You only speak to the examiner. You don't speak to the other student.

© Cambridge University Press and UCLES 2015

Go to https://www.youtube.com/user/cambridgeenglishtv to watch official Cambridge English videos of *Key* and *Key for Schools* Speaking tests.

Daily life

1 Complete the conversation with the words in the box.

afternoon	evening	meeting
morning	o'clock	past	quarter
tomorrow	Tuesday	week

Matt: Hi Maria. I haven't seen you for ages! Are you going to Peter's party this **(1)** .... ? I think it starts at eight **(2)** ....

Maria: No, I have to study tonight because I've got an important maths exam **(3)** ....

Matt: Oh, okay. Good luck!

Maria: Thanks. My exams finish next week so do you want to play tennis on **(4)** .... ?

Matt: I can't. I'm **(5)** .... Martin to talk about our summer holiday.

Maria: What time are you meeting him?

Matt: At a **(6)** .... to ten. He starts work at midday.

Maria: Why don't we play tennis in the **(7)** .... ? We could meet outside the sports centre at half **(8)** .... four.

Matt: Great! But can you lend me a racket? Mine is broken.

Maria: No problem! See you next **(9)** .... and have fun at the party! Do you want me to phone you in the **(10)** .... , after my exam?

Matt: No!! I'll be sleeping!

☑ Exam task

2 Use the words to make complete questions or sentences. Ask and answer with a partner.

1. What | name?
2. And | what | surname?
3. How | you | spell ?
4. Who | dinner | your | house?
5. time | you | get | up?
6. Where | usually | lunch?
7. What | wear | weekend?
8. When | meet | friends?
9. Where | do | English | homework?
10. like | playing | computer | games?
11. Tell | something | last weekend.
12. Tell | something | about | favourite | sport.

3 Put the words in the correct order to make sentences.

1. early / never / get up / I / at / the weekend / .

....

2. reads / brother / My / comics / always / .

....

3. often / on / pizza / We / Saturdays / eat / .

....

4. is / sunny / in / It / the summer / usually / .

....

5. English / always / classes / I / on Mondays / have / .

....

6. I / tired / the evening / in / sometimes / am / .

....

7. at / I / the house / usually / leave / half past eight / .

....

8. rides / dad / a motorbike / My / sometimes / to work / .

....

9. the / never / do / cooking / I / at home / .

....

10. in / I / often / my friends / meet / the evening / .

....

☑ **Exam tips**

- Answer with more than one word. For example, if the examiner asks you 'Where do you come from?', say 'I come from Italy' and not just 'Italy'.
- For the last question, the examiner will ask you to speak about one thing. For example, he or she will say: 'Tell me about your family' or 'Tell me about your hobbies'.
- Try to say three things when you answer the *Tell me about ...* question.

Go to https://www.youtube.com/user/cambridgeenglishtv to watch official Cambridge English videos of *Key* and *Key for Schools* Speaking tests.

Places and buildings

1 **Choose the correct word to complete the conversation, a, b or c.**

1. Have you bought your ticket to York yet?

No, but my dad is driving me to the .... to get it this afternoon.

a cinema   **b** museum   **c** bus station

2. What do you do at the weekends?

I love dancing so I always go to the .... on Fridays.

a supermarket   **b** disco   **c** theatre

3. Where do you usually meet your friends?

We often spend the whole day in the .... , but we never buy anything!

a library   **b** shopping centre **c** park

4. Have you finished writing your postcards yet?

Yes, and now I need to buy some stamps. Where's the .... ?

a department store **b** museum   **c** post office

5. What are you doing tomorrow afternoon?

I'm having a surfing lesson at 3 pm with my friend at the ....

a beach   **b** sports centre   **c** swimming pool

6. How often do you go to the .... ?

I usually go every Friday.

a supermarket   **b** café   **c** hotel

7. What's your favourite film?

I don't like films. I prefer watching plays at the ....

a theatre   **b** school   **c** gallery

8. Where do you do sport?

I usually go running in the .... every afternoon.

a swimming pool   **b** park   **c** shopping centre

9. Do you like reading books?

Yes, I do. I borrow books from the .... every month.

a bookshop   **b** library   **c** bank

10. Tell me about your best friend.

Her name's Rosie and she's a nurse. She works in a ....

a school   **b** pharmacy   **c** hospital

 **Exam task**

2

Complete the questions and sentences. Ask and answer with a partner.

1. What's .... name?
2. And .... your surname?
3. How do you .... that?
4. .... do you go at the weekend?
5. Where .... tourists visit in your country?
6. Is .... a swimming pool near your house?
7. How .... parks are there in your town?

8. Where do you .... shopping?
9. .... often do you watch TV?
10. What's the most beautiful place in .... town?
11. Tell me something .... your favourite place in your town.
12. .... something about your house / flat.

3

Match the questions with the answers.

1. Do you like going to the theatre? ....
2. How often do you go the cinema? ....
3. When do you usually do sport? ....
4. What do you usually do with your friends? ....
5. Where did you go yesterday afternoon? ....
6. How often do you to the library? ....
7. When do you go shopping? ....
8. How often do you watch sport on TV? ....

a Every day! I swim one kilometre every morning.

b Every Saturday! I usually go with my sister and she always buys some new clothes.

c I sometimes go there to study but I never borrow books.

d I went to the art gallery. There were a lot of tourists but I loved the paintings. Dali's were my favourite.

e Never! I always go to the stadium to watch my favourite team.

f Never, because it's very expensive. I like watching films on my computer.

g We love cooking so we usually go to the supermarket to get the food and then we make dinner together.

h Yes, I do. I love watching plays.

Get it right!

Look at the sentence below. Then try to correct the mistake.

What time you can come?

Go to https://www.youtube.com/user/cambridgeenglishtv to watch official Cambridge English videos of *Key* and *Key for Schools* Speaking tests.

Hobbies and leisure

1 Match the questions with the answers.

1.	What time do you leave the house in the morning?
2.	Do you wear a uniform for work?
3.	When do you watch TV?
4.	What did you have for breakfast this morning?
5.	Do you listen to the radio?
6.	Where do you usually have dinner?
7.	How often do you send emails?
8.	Who do you play sport with?

a	At home, with my family.
b	Every day, because I work in an office.
c	Some toast and a glass of orange juice.
d	Usually around half past eight.
e	In the evening, after dinner.
f	No, I don't. I prefer listening to my MP3 player.
g	My friends, we usually go to the gym or the swimming pool.
h	Yes, I do, because I'm a waitress.

☑ Exam task

2 Candidate A, here is some information about painting lessons. Candidate B, you don't know anything about the painting lessons, so go to page 97 and ask A some questions about them. Now B, ask your questions about the painting lessons and A, you answer them.

Candidate A – your answers

Painting lessons

Class start: 11th January

Ten week course: £25

Our groups are very small (five people!)

"Joanna Jackson is a fantastic teacher!"

More information: ☎ 245932

Candidate A – your questions

Appleton Castle

- student's ticket £?
- buy / food?
- what / see?
- open / Sunday?
- where / castle?

Candidate B, here is some information about a castle. Candidate A, you don't know anything about the castle, so go to page 96 and ask B some questions about it. Now A, ask your questions about the castle and B, you answer them.

Candidate B – your answers

Appleton Castle

Visit us on Treetop Hill.

Enjoy our beautiful garden and museum.

Open 9:30 am – 5.30 pm (closed Sundays)

Tickets: Adults £10 Students £5

New! Buy sandwiches and drinks in our café.

Candidate B – your questions

Painting lessons

- cost?
- name / teacher?
- when / start?
- big classes?
- telephone number?

---

3 Put the letters in the correct order to make months and seasons.

1. Aguuts ....
2. tmuanu ....
3. Dmebeecr ....
4. Fbreruya ....
5. Jyaanru ....

6. yJlu ....
7. bSempetre ....
8. sipgrn ....
9. smuemr ....
10. rweitn ....

 Exam facts

- In this part, you talk to the other student.
- You have to read some notes and then ask and answer five questions about them.
- You only speak to the other student. You don't speak to the examiner.

© Cambridge University Press and UCLES 2015

Go to https://www.youtube.com/user/cambridgeenglishtv to watch official Cambridge English videos of *Key* and *Key for Schools* Speaking tests.

Sports

1 Complete the sentences with the correct word from the box.

cycle	go	hit	kick	practise	ride	swim	throw	watch	win

1. When you play basketball, you catch the ball and .... it to the other players.
2. Next year I'm going to learn to .... a horse.
3. You have to .... the ball with a bat when you play cricket.
4. If you want to be good at sport, you have to .... every day.
5. You must be able to .... if you want to learn to surf.
6. Many people prefer to .... sport on TV at the weekend.
7. I want to .... around the city on my new bike tomorrow.
8. You mustn't .... the ball when you play volleyball.
9. I love playing tennis but I never .... my matches.
10. In the summer, I usually .... running on the beach.

☑ Exam tips

- Look at the title and picture on the card and read the notes carefully.
- Asking questions: you must ask all five questions.
- Answering questions: only use the information from your notes. Do not add any other information.
- If you don't understand what the other student says, ask him or her to say it again.

☑ Exam task

2 Candidate A, here is some information about a surfing competition. Candidate B, you don't know anything about the surfing competition, so go to page 99 and ask A some questions about it. Now B, ask your questions about the surfing competition, and A, you answer them.

Candidate A – your answers

> <u>Surfing competition!</u>
>
>
>
> Saturday 15th September at 2 pm
>
> South Beach (in front of the café)
>
> All ages welcome!
>
> Entry: £5 (price includes a t-shirt).
>
> 1st Prize: digital camera

Candidate A – your questions

> <u>Tennis lessons</u>
> - Where?
> - More information?
> - Advanced class / 6:15 pm?
> - Every day?
> - Cost?

Candidate B, here is some information about tennis lessons. Candidate A, you don't know anything about the tennis lessons, so go to page 98 and ask B some questions about them. Now A, ask your questions about the tennis lessons, and B, you answer them.

Candidate B – your answers

Candidate B – your questions

> ### Tennis lessons
>
> Make friends and get fit!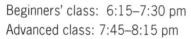
>
> In City Park every Tuesday and Thursday
>
> Beginners' class: 6:15–7:30 pm
> Advanced class: 7:45–8:15 pm
>
> £28.50 every month
>
> Excellent teachers!
>
> Find out more at www.playtennis.com

> ### Surfing competition!
>
> • for adults?
> • what / win?
> • where?
> • when / competition?
> • cost / enter?

3a **Put the words in the correct order to make questions. Then read the poster and answer the questions.**

1. the / Where / club / is / sports / ? ....
....

2. go / Can / in / I / June / ? ....
....

3. Fridays / Are / lessons / on / there / ? ....
....

4. find / How / I / information / can / more / ? ....
....

5. the / How / lessons / do / much / cost / ? ....
....

6. go / can / Who / to / club / the / sports / ? ....
....

> ### Summer Sports club!
>
> For everyone who loves sport!
> Learn to play volleyball, basketball and hockey and more!
> Blackstone Park
> Monday–Friday 1 July to 31 August.
> Lessons cost £10 for two hours.
> For more information: Contact: Peter on 7532456

3b **Now practise the dialogue with a partner.**

Go to https://www.youtube.com/user/cambridgeenglishtv to watch official Cambridge English videos of *Key* and *Key for Schools* Speaking tests.

Travel and holidays

1a Put the words in the correct place in the table.

boat	bridge	bus stop	car	catch	drive
driver	helicopter	passenger	roundabout	taxi	
tourist	traffic light	travel	visit	visitor	

A thing	A person	A way to travel	A verb
....	....	....	....
....	....	....	....
....	....	....	....
....	....	....	....

1b Complete the sentences with a word from Exercise 1a. You do not need to use all the words.

1. Lots of visitors to London take a .... trip on the River Thames.
2. I took a .... ride over the Grand Canyon last year – it was fantastic.
3. Often, it is faster to .... by train than by bus.
4. I usually go to work on the bus because there's a .... at the end of my street.
5. You have to stop when a .... is red.
6. In the UK you can learn to .... when you are 17 years old.

☑ Exam task

2 Candidate A, here is some information about a day trip to a local town. Candidate B, you don't know anything about the day trip to the local town, so go to page 101 and ask A some questions about it. Now B, ask A your questions about the day trip to the local town and A, you answer them.

Candidate A – your answers

Day trip

Visit Bridgetown every Saturday.

Tour of old town with local guide.

Explore the castle and shop in the local market.

Hungry? Have lunch in Fin's fish restaurant!

Price: £35 (including train tickets and guided tour)

Candidate A – your questions

Best Buys Travel Agents

- Open / Saturday?
- Expensive?
- Where?
- Phone number?
- go / USA?

Candidate B, here is some information about a travel agents. Candidate A, you don't know anything about the travel agents, so go to page 100 and ask B some questions about them. Now A, ask B your questions about the travel agents and B, you answer them.

Candidate B – your answers

Candidate B – your questions

Best Buys Travel Agents	
Come and see us on Summerfield Street, Hillford. 	

We've got cheap holidays for you and your family!

Open 9:30 am–5 pm Monday–Friday
(Saturday: 9:30–1 pm)

New this year! Holidays in the USA and Mexico.

Tel: 6785430

Day trip
- guided tour?
- when / go?
- what / do?
- day trip / cost?
- where / eat?

---

3 Complete the text with the correct words, a, b or c.

My name's Joshua and I love travelling. I've been to lots places and I've **(1)** .... some amazing people. Actually, last year, I even **(2)** .... a famous actor on the beach in Mexico!
This year I've already **(3)** .... three countries. In January, I saw my sister in Spain, in March, I **(4)** .... to Italy and I've just **(5)** .... home from a holiday with my friends. It was fun but my bag **(6)** .... in the supermarket near our hotel!
This summer I **(7)** .... to California with my cousin. We **(8)** .... a motorbike along Highway One and explore San Francisco. I think we **(9)** .... an amazing time!

1. **a** have met   **b** meet   **c** met
2. **a** seen   **b** saw   **c** see
3. **a** visit   **b** visited   **c** visiting
4. **a** go   **b** gone   **c** went
5. **a** return   **b** returned   **c** returning
6. **a** stole   **b** has stolen   **c** was stolen
7. **a** am going   **b** go   **c** will go
8. **a** are going to ride **b** ride   **c** 'll ride
9. **a** had   **b** have   **c** 'll have

Get it right!

Look at the sentences below and and choose the correct one.

Write me a letter to tell me what **are you** going to do.

Write me a letter to tell me what **you are** going to do.

Go to https://www.youtube.com/user/cambridgeenglishtv to watch official Cambridge English videos of *Key* and *Key for Schools* Speaking tests.

Think about it — Key Reading and Writing Part 1

Read about Key Reading and Writing Part 1. Are the sentences TRUE or FALSE?

1. In this part of the exam I have to match notices with the correct meaning. ....

2. All of the words in the notices will be from the Key vocabulary list. ....

3. There are two sentences for each notice. ....

4. For each question, I only need to mark the correct letter on my answer sheet. ....

5. There are eight notices in total. ....

6. I need to understand the main message of each notice. ....

7. I can use letters more than once if I need to. ....

8. There is an example at the beginning of Key Reading and Writing Part 1. ....

Think about it — Key Reading and Writing Part 2

Complete the sentences about Key Reading and Writing Part 2 with the correct alternatives.

1. There are *five / six* sentences in Part 2, not including the example.

2. *Most / All* of the sentences are about the same person, or the same subject.

3. Each sentence has a *word / two words* missing.

4. *Under / Above* each sentence there are three options; A, B and C.

5. On the answer sheet, you have to write the *missing word / the correct letter* for each question.

6. The words in Part 2 are *all / not all* on the Key vocabulary list.

7. Part 2 is a test of *grammar / vocabulary*.

8. The story makes it *more difficult / easier* to choose the correct answer.

 **Think about it**   Key Reading and Writing Part 3

Complete each sentence about Key Reading and Writing Part 3 Sections 1 and 2 with a number from the box.

one (x2)   two   three   five (x3)   eight

Section 1

1. There are .... short conversations in the first section of Key Reading and Writing Part 3.

2. For each question, there are .... possible answers to choose from.

Section 2

3. There is .... conversation in the second section of Key Reading and Writing Part 3.

4. The conversation is between .... people.

5. There are .... gaps in the conversation.

6. You have to complete the conversation by choosing from a total of .... sentences.

7. You only need to use .... of the sentences.

Sections 1 and 2

8. You will see .... example at the beginning of both sections of Key Reading and Writing Part 3.

 **Think about it**   Key Reading and Writing Part 4

Complete the information about Key Reading and Writing Part 4 with the correct alternatives.

Key Reading and Writing Part 4 is a **(1)** *reading / writing* exercise. Sometimes you will be asked to read three short texts, and sometimes it is one longer text. The number of words you have to read is **(2)** *always / not always* the same. There might be **(3)** *lots of / a few words* in the text which are not in the KEY vocabulary list, **(4)** *and you will / but you won't* need to understand these words to answer the questions correctly. There are seven questions to answer, with three possible answers for each question: **(5)** *(A, B or C) / (1, 2 or 3)*.

If there is one long text to read, there are two types of multiple-choice questions:

i) Seven **(6)** *long / short* questions, each with three possible short answers.

ii) Seven short sentences about the text. You have to decide if each sentence is true, false, or if the information isn't given in the text. With this type of question, the answer will be **(7)** *don't know / not given*.

If there are three short texts to read, they will be labelled with the **(8)** *name / number* of the person in the text. You will read seven short questions and decide which text gives the answer.

 **Think about it** Key Reading and Writing Part 5

Read the following sentences about KEY Reading and Writing Part 5. Are the sentences TRUE or FALSE?

1. Key Reading and Writing Part 5 is a writing exercise. ....

2. There are five questions to answer. ....

3. You have to choose the correct word for each gap in a text. ....

4. There are four possible answers for each gap. ....

5. The text might be information from an encyclopaedia, or a news story. ....

6. This part of the Reading and Writing exam tests vocabulary. ....

7. There is an example to help you to understand the exercise. ....

8. Example answer words are prepositions, modal verbs and conjunctions. ....

 **Think about it** Key Reading and Writing Part 6

| dictionary | first | group | line | list | sentences | spelling | verbs |

Complete the sentences about Key Reading and Writing Part 6 with the words in the box.

1. Key Reading and Writing Part 6 is a test of vocabulary and ....

2. In Part 6, you have to read five short .... and write the word which each one defines.

3. The definitions are like those you can find in a ....

4. You are given the .... letter of each word to help you.

5. There is a dash (a short ....) for each missing letter.

6. The words can be nouns, ... or adjectives.

7. All of the words go together in a .... For example, words about sport, or things you find in a kitchen.

8. All of the words in Part 6 are in the Key vocabulary ....

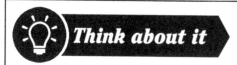 **Think about it** Key Reading and Writing Part 7

Complete the sentences about Key Reading and Writing Part 7 with the verbs in the box.

answer	choose	fill	read	show	spell	think	write

In Key Reading and Writing Part 7, you have to **(1)** .... a short text or two short texts, and **(2)** .... in the gaps. The texts will usually be emails, letters, or notes. If there are two texts, the second will be a response to the first. For example, the first text might be an invitation, and the second text will **(3)** .... that invitation. There are ten gaps to fill in, plus an example to **(4)** .... you what to do. There are no words to **(5)** .... from – you have to **(6)** .... of the missing word. You should **(7)** .... only one word in each gap, and you must **(8)** .... the word correctly. Part 7 tests grammar, and the missing words will usually be auxiliary verbs, modal verbs, prepositions, pronouns or determiners.

 **Think about it** Key Reading and Writing Part 8

Complete the sentences about Key Reading and Writing Part 8 with the words in the box.

answers	days	diary	one	posters	price	three	spelling

Key Reading and Writing Part 8 is a reading and writing exercise. You have to read two short texts in order to find the answers. The short texts might be emails, advertisements, **(1)** .... or notices. The part you have to complete is someone's notes or their **(2)** .... You have to find information such as times, **(3)** .... , names, etc. The answers will be one word, two words or a number (which might be a time, a date or a **(4)** .... It is very important to copy the words exactly, with the correct **(5)** .... Remember that some of the **(6)** .... will be in one of the texts, and some will be in the other text. Read both texts carefully to make sure you are writing the correct information. If you are asked for a date, for example, there may be two or **(7)** .... dates in the texts. Make sure you choose the correct **(8)** ....

 **Think about it**   Key Reading and Writing Part 9

Match the questions about Key Reading and Writing Part 9 with the answers.

1. Is Key Reading and Writing Part 9 a reading or a writing exercise?

2. What type of message do I write?

3. What information do I need to include?

4. What if I don't answer all the questions?

5. How long should my answer be?

a The instructions will say if you should write a short letter, an email or a postcard.

b You must answer all of the questions to get full marks.

c It is a writing task.

d There will be three short questions. You should answer all of them in your piece of writing.

e You must write between 25 and 35 words.

 **Think about it**   Key Listening Part 1

Match 1–8 with a–h to make sentences about Key Listening Part 1.

1. In Key Listening Part 1, there are

2. Every question has

3. You have to

4. You will hear a conversation

5. The conversations may be between friends or relatives,

6. You need to listen for important information, such as

7. You will hear

8. You need to choose and write your answers

a or a shop assistant and a customer, for example.

b between two people.

c choose one answer for each question; A, B or C.

d five questions.

e three answer options, based on pictures.

f each conversation twice.

g times, prices, days of the week or numbers.

h while you are listening to the conversations.

 **Key Listening Part 2**

Complete the information about Key Listening Part 2 with the words in the box.

activities	answer	daily	eight	end	five	question	simple	twice	two

In Key Listening Part 2 you need to understand a **(1)** .... conversation between **(2)** .... people.

They might be talking about topics such as free time **(3)** .... , travel or **(4)** .... life. You will hear

the conversation **(5)** .... There are **(6)** .... questions and you have to choose from **(7)** ....

options. You should write your answers on the **(8)** .... paper while you listen and you have time at the

(9) .... of the listening test to write your answers onto the **(10)** .... sheet in pencil.

Key Listening Part 3

Read the sentences about Key Listening Part 3 and choose the correct alternatives.

1. In Key Listening Part 3, you answer the questions by *choosing A, B or C / writing a word.*

2. You listen to *one long conversation / five short conversations.*

3. You listen to *two / four* people talking.

4. There are *five / eight* questions to answer.

5. The speakers *know / don't know* each other.

6. The speakers talk about *school, university or work / something they are interested in.*

7. You must choose *one answer / two answers* for each question.

8. You are given *one point / two points* for every correct answer.

 **Think about it** Key Listening Part 4

Read the sentences about Key Listening Part 4. Are the answers TRUE or FALSE?

1. In Key Listening Part 4, you will hear two people talking. ....

2. The speakers will always have a British accent. ....

3. You will complete a message or notes with information. ....

4. You need to choose from A, B or C answers. ....

5. The answer will always be one word. ....

6. You can make spelling mistakes in this part of the exam. ....

7. There are five gaps to complete in a text. ....

8. The speakers might spell some of the difficult words. ....

 **Think about it** Key Listening Part 5

Read the paragraph about Key Listening part 5 and answer the questions.

In Part 5 of the Key Listening test, you have to answer five questions. You will hear one person giving information about something. The information you are listening for might be a date, a time or a name, for example. The speaker might spell some words (for example the name of a street) and you must write these correctly. You need to write one or more words for each answer and you will hear the information twice. You should write on the question paper while you are listening. You will then have eight minutes to complete the answer paper at the end of the test.

1. How many questions are there in Key Listening Part 5?

2. How many speakers will there be?

3. What sort of information might you hear?

4. Will the speaker spell any words in Part 5?

5. How many words do you need to write for each answer?

6. Where do you have to write your answers while you are listening?

 **Think about it** Key Speaking Part 1

Read the paragraph about Key Speaking Part 1 and answer the questions with the words in the box. You do not need to use all the words.

In Key Speaking Part 1 you need to listen to the examiner and answer their questions. You will have to spell your surname and talk about yourself. For example the examiner might ask you about your interests, your town or your family. There will be another student (or maybe two) in the room too, but in this part of the speaking test you only need to talk to the examiner. There will be two examiners in the room too. One of them will talk to the students and the other one will only listen to you both. You should always try to use good vocabulary and grammar in the speaking test but it is okay to make some mistakes! Key Speaking Part 1 lasts 5–6 minutes.

| five to six   nationality   no   surname   the examiner   the other student   two   yes   yourself |

1. Will the examiner give you a card with questions on it? ....
2. What will you have to spell? Your ....
3. What will you talk about? ....
4. Who will you talk to? ....
5. How many speaking examiners will there be? ....
6. How long is this part of the Key exam? .... minutes

---

 **Think about it** Key Speaking Part 2

Read the text. Then match the questions about the Key Speaking test Part 2 with the answers.

In the second part of the speaking test you have to talk to another student. You will have to ask and answer questions but you do not have to give personal information about yourself. The examiner will give you a card with some information on it. The information might be about daily life, hobbies or free times activities. You have to look at the card and answer the other student's questions. For example, your card might have information about a new club or a competition and your partner might ask you questions about times, places or prices on it. You have to find the answers on your card and tell the other student what they are. Later, the examiner will give you a different card and you will ask the other student some questions. This part of the test takes about three or four minutes.

1. Who do you have to talk to?
2. Do you have to give information about yourself?
3. Do you have to ask questions or answer questions?
4. What will the examiner give you?
5. How do you know what to ask your partner?
6. Where can you find the answer to your partner's questions?

a   A card with information or questions ideas on it.
b   The other student.
c   Both of them.
d   You need to use the words on your card to help you make questions.
e   No, you don't.
f   On your information card.

Appliances

camera	DVD (player)	laptop	telephone
CD (player)	electric	lights	television / TV
cell phone	electricity	mobile (phone)	video
clock	fridge	MP3 player	washing machine
computer	gas	PC	
cooker	heating	phone	
digital camera	lamp	radio	

Clothes and Accessories

bag	fashion	raincoat	tights
bathing suit	glasses	ring	trainers
belt	glove	scarf	trousers
blouse	handbag	shirt	try on (v)
boot	hat	shoes	T-shirt
bracelet	jacket	shorts	umbrella
cap	jeans	skirt	uniform
chain	jewellery / jewelry	suit	wallet
clothes	jumper	sunglasses	watch
coat	kit	sweater	wear (v)
costume (swimming)	necklace	swimming costume	
dress	pocket	swimsuit	
earring	purse	tie	

Colours

black	golden	orange	red
blue	green	pale	white
brown	grey	pink	yellow
dark	light	purple	

Communication and Technology

address	cell phone	digital camera	file
at / @	chat	dot	information
by post	click (v)	download (n & v)	internet
call (v)	computer	DVD (player)	keyboard
camera	conversation	email (n & v)	laptop (computer)
CD (player)	digital	envelope	mobile (phone)

mouse	phone	software	web
MP3 player	photograph	talk	web page
net	photography	telephone	website
online	printer	text (n & v)	
PC	screen	video	

Documents and Texts

ad / advertisement	diary	magazine	passport
article	diploma	menu	postcard
bill	email	message	project
book	form	newspaper	text (n & v)
card	letter	note	textbook
comic	licence	notebook	ticket

Education

advanced	course	lesson	ruler
beginner	desk	level	school
biology	dictionary	library	science
blackboard	diploma	mark	student
board	eraser	maths/mathematics	studies
book	exam(ination)	note	study (v)
bookshelf	geography	physics	subject
chemistry	history	practice (n)	teach
class	homework	practise (v)	teacher
classmate	information	project	term
classroom	instructions	pupil	test (n)
clever	know	read	university
coach	language	remember	
college	learn	rubber	

Entertainment and Media

act	card	dance (n & v)	festival
actor	cartoon	dancer	film (n & v)
adventure	CD (player)	disco	fun
advertisement	chess	draw	go out
art	cinema	drawing	group
article	classical (music)	drum	guitar
board game	competition	DVD (player)	hip hop
book	concert	exhibition	instrument

keyboard	newspaper	pop (music)	sing
laugh	opera	practice **(n)**	singer
listen to	paint **(v)**	practise **(v)**	song
look at	painter	programme	television / TV
magazine	photograph	project	theatre
MP3 player	photographer	radio	ticket
museum	photography	read **(v)**	video (game)
music	piano	rock (concert)	watch **(v)**
musician	picture	screen **(n)**	
news	play **(n)**	show **(n)**	

Family and Friends

aunt	girl	group	mum(my)
boy	grandchild	guest	neighbour
brother	grand(d)ad	guy	parent
child	granddaughter	husband	pen-friend
cousin	grandfather	love **(n & v)**	sister
dad(dy)	grandma	married	son
daughter	grandmother	Miss	surname
family	grandpa	mother	teenager
father	grandparent	Mr	uncle
friend	grandson	Mrs	wife
friendly	granny	Ms	

Food and Drink

apple	butter	coffee	fish
bake	cafe/café	cola	food
banana	cafeteria	cook **(n & v)**	fork
barbecue	cake	cooker	fridge
biscuit	can **(n)**	cream	fried
boil	candy	cup	fruit
boiled	carrot	curry	garlic
bottle	cereal	cut **(n)**	glass
bowl	cheese	dessert	grape
box	chef	dinner	grilled
bread	chicken	dish **(n)**	honey
break **(n)**	chilli	drink	hungry
breakfast	chips	eat	ice
burger	chocolate	egg	ice cream

jam	mineral water	potato	sweet **(n & adj)**
juice	mushroom	rice	tea
kitchen	oil	roast **(v & adj)**	thirsty
knife	omelette	salad	toast
lemon	onion	salt	tomato
lemonade	orange	sandwich	vegetable
lunch	pasta	sauce	waiter
main course	pear	sausage	waitress
meal	pepper	slice **(n)**	wash up
meat	picnic	snack **(n)**	yog(h)urt
melon	piece of cake	soup	
menu	pizza	steak	
milk	plate	sugar	

Health, Medicine and Exercise

accident	cut **(v)**	foot	pain
ambulance	danger	hair	problem
appointment	dangerous	hand	rest **(n)**
arm	dead	head	run
baby	dentist	health	sick
back	die	hear **(v)**	soap
bandage	doctor	heart	stomach
blood	Dr	hospital	stomach ache
body	ear	hurt **(v)**	swim
brain	exercise	ill	temperature
break **(v)**	eye	leg	tired
check **(v)**	face	lie down	tooth
chemist	fall **(v)**	medicine	toothache
clean **(adj & v)**	feel **(v)**	neck	toothbrush
cold **(n)**	finger	nose	walk
comb **(n)**	fit	nurse	well **(adj)**

Hobbies and Leisure

barbecue	camp	computer	guitar
beach	camping	dance **(n & v)**	hobby
bicycle	campsite	draw	holidays
bike	CD (player)	DVD (player)	join
book	club	festival	magazine
camera	collect **(v)**	go out	member

MP3 player	musician	party	quiz
museum	paint (n & v)	photograph (n & v)	tent
music	park	picnic	video game

House and Home

address	computer	garage	refrigerator
apartment	cooker	garden	roof
armchair	cupboard	gas	room
bath(tub)	curtain	gate	safe (adj)
bathroom	desk	hall	shelf
bed	dining room	heating	shower
bedroom	door	home	sink
blanket	downstairs	house	sitting room
bookcase	drawer	key	sofa
bookshelf	DVD (player)	kitchen	stay (v)
bowl	entrance	lamp	toilet
box	flat (n)	light	towel
carpet	floor	live (v)	
chair	fridge	living room	
clock	furniture	pillow	

Measurements

centimetre / centimeter	half	litre / liter	second
	hour	metre / meter	temperature
day	kilo(gram[me])/kg	minute	week
degree	kilometre/km/ kilometer	moment	year
gram(me)		quarter	

Personal Feelings, Opinions and Experiences (adjectives)

able	bored	different	funny
afraid	boring	difficult	good
alone	brave	excellent	great
amazing	brilliant	famous	happy
angry	busy	fast	hard
bad	careful	favourite	heavy
beautiful	clear	fine	high
better	clever	free	hungry
big	cool	friendly	important

interested	pleasant	small	tired
interesting	poor	soft	unhappy
kind	pretty	sorry	useful
lovely	quick	special	well
lucky	quiet	strange	worried
married	ready	strong	wrong
modern	real	sure	young
nice	rich	sweet	
noisy	right	tall	
old	slow	terrible	

Places: Buildings

apartment (building)	college	hospital	school
bank	department store	hotel	shop
block	disco	house	sports centre
bookshop	elevator	library	stadium
bookstore	entrance	lift	supermarket
building	exit	museum	swimming pool
cafe/café	factory	office	theatre
cafeteria	flat	pharmacy	university
castle	garage	police station	
cathedral	grocery store	post office	
cinema	guest-house	railway station	

Places: Countryside

area	forest	path	sky
beach	hill	railway	village
campsite	island	rainforest	wood
farm	lake	river	
field	mountain	sea	

Places: Town and City

airport	city centre	petrol station	station
bridge	corner	playground	street
bus station	market	road	town
bus stop	motorway	roundabout	underground
car park	park	square	zoo

Services

bank	doctor	petrol station	theatre
cafe / café	garage	post office	tourist information
cafeteria	hotel	restaurant	
cinema	library	sports centre	
dentist	museum	swimming pool	

Shopping

ad / advertisement	cheque	expensive	shop
assistant	close (v)	for sale	shop assistant
bill	closed	open (v & adj)	shopper
bookshop	cost (n & v)	pay (for)	shopping
buy (v)	credit card	penny	spend
cash (n & v)	customer	pound	store
cent	department store	price	supermarket
change (n & v)	dollar	receipt	try on
cheap	euro	rent	

Sport

ball	football	riding	swimming
badminton	football player	rugby	swimming costume
baseball	game	run (v)	swimming pool
basketball	goal	sailing	swimsuit
bat	golf	sea	table tennis
bathing suit	hockey	skate (v)	team
beach	kit	skateboard (n)	tennis
bicycle	luck	ski (v)	tennis player
bike	member	skiing	throw (v)
boat	play (v)	snowboard (n)	ticket
catch (v)	player pool	snowboarding	tired
climb (v)	(n) practice	soccer	trainers
club	(n) practise	sport(s)	v / versus
coach (n)	(v) prize	sports centre	volleyball
competition	race (n & v)	stadium	walk (v)
cricket	racket	surf	watch (v)
cycling	rest (n & v)	surfboard	win (v)
enter (a competition)	ride (n & v)	surfboarding	windsurfing
fishing		swim	winner

The Natural World

air	fire	moon	spring
autumn	flower	mountain	star
beach	forest	north	summer
bee	grass	plant	tree
country	grow	rabbit	water
countryside	hill	river	west
desert	hot	sea	winter
east	ice	sky	wood
explorer	island	south	wool
field	lake	space	world

Time

afternoon	evening	morning	tonight
a.m./p.m.	half (past)	night	week
appointment	holidays	noon	weekday
autumn	hour	o'clock	weekend
birthday	January - December	past	weekly
calendar	meeting	quarter (past/to)	winter
century	midnight	second	working hours
clock	minute	spring	year
daily	moment	summer	yesterday
date	Monday - Sunday	time	
day	month	today	
diary	monthly	tomorrow	

Travel and Transport

(aero)/(air)plane	country	fly	miss (v)
airport	delay (n & v)	garage	motorbike
ambulance	delayed	helicopter	motorway
backpack	drive	journey	move
boat	driver	leave	oil
bridge	driving/driver's	left	park (v)
bus	licence	light	passenger
bus station	engine	luggage	passport
bus stop	engineer	machine	petrol
car	explorer	map	petrol station
case	far	mechanic	pilot
coach	flight	mirror	platform

railway
repair (v)
return (n & v)
ride
right
road
roundabout
sailing
seat

ship
station
stop
straight on
street
suitcase
taxi
ticket
tour (n)

tour guide
tourist
tourist information
    centre
traffic
traffic light
tram
travel
trip

tyre
underground (n)
visit
visitor
way (n)
wheel
window

Weather

cloud
cloudy
cold
fog
foggy

hot
ice
rain
snow
storm

sun
sunny
thunderstorm
warm
weather

wet
wind
windy

Work and Jobs

actor
artist
boss
break (n)
business
businessman
businesswoman
chemist
cleaner
coach (n)
company
computer
cook (n & v)
customer
dentist
desk
diary

diploma
doctor
Dr
driver
earn
email (n & v)
engineer
explorer
factory
farm
farmer
footballer
football player
guest
guide
instructions
job

journalist
king
letter
manager
mechanic
meeting
message
musician
nurse
occupation
office
painter
photographer
pilot
police officer
queen
receptionist

secretary
shop assistant
shopper
singer
staff
student
teacher
tennis player
tour guide
uniform
waiter/ waitress
work
worker
writer

ACKNOWLEDGEMENTS

Development of this publication has made use of the Cambridge English Corpus, a multi-billion word collection of spoken and written English. It includes the Cambridge Learner Corpus, a unique collection of candidate exam answers. Cambridge University Press has built up the Cambridge English Corpus to provide evidence about language use that helps to produce better language teaching materials.

The authors and publishers acknowledge the following sources of copyright material and are grateful for the permissions granted. While every effort has been made, it has not always been possible to identify the sources of all the material used, or to trace all copyright holders. If any omissions are brought to our notice, we will be happy to include the appropriate acknowledgements on reprinting and in the next update to the digital edition, as applicable.

p. 6: Wavebreakmedia Ltd/Getty Images; p. 9: Glowimages/Getty Images; p. 12: Michael Krasowitz/Photographer's Choice/Getty Images; p. 14: Verdina Anna/Moment/Getty Images; p. 17: Janine Lamontagne/E+/Getty Images; p. 19: Jamie Grill/Iconica/Getty Images; p. 21: jeffbergen/E+/Getty Images; p. 23: Johnny Louis/WireImage/Getty Images; p. 25: Martyn Ferry/Moment/Getty Images; p. 26: Caiaimage/Chris Ryan/OJO+/Getty Images; p. 28: Peter Durant/Passage/Getty Images; p. 30: Jupiterimages/Stockbyte/Getty Images; p. 32: 8213erika/iStock/Getty Images; p. 34: Kenny Bengtsson/Folio/Getty Images; p. 36: A L Christensen/Moment Open/Getty Images; p. 38: Riitta Supperi/Folio Images/Getty Images; p. 40: Sam Edwards/Caiaimage/Getty Images; p. 42: Andersen Ross/DigitalVision/Getty Images; p. 45: Erik Isakson/Getty Images; p. 46: Geri Lavrov/Moment Open/Getty Images; p. 48: John Lund/Paula Zacharias/Blend Images/Getty Images; p. 50: blue jean images/Getty Images; p. 53: ClaudioVentrella/iStock/Getty Images; p. 55: BraunS/E+/Getty Images; p. 56: Steve Debenport/E+/Getty Images; p. 59: John Eder/Stone/Getty Images; p. 66: Jovanmandic/iStock/Getty Images; p. 68: Don Mason/Blend Images/Getty Images; p. 70: Colin Hawkins/Cultura/Getty Images; p. 72: Howard Kingsnorth/Cultura Exclusive/Getty Images; p. 74: monkeybusinessimages/iStock/Getty Images; p. 76: m-imagephotography/iStock/Getty Images; p. 79: Marco Simoni/robertharding/Getty Images; p. 80: Martin Barraud/OJO Images/Getty Images; p. 83: PeopleImages.com/DigitalVision/Getty Images; p. 84: Spaces Images/Blend Images/Getty Images; p. 87: Tim Mosenfelder/Getty Images Entertainment/Getty Images; p. 88: Robert Nickelsberg/Getty Images News/Getty Images; p. 90: Image Source/Getty Images; p. 92: i love images/Cultura/Getty Images; p. 94: Diane Auckland/Passage/Getty Images.

Illustrations by Nigel Dobbyn

The publishers are grateful to the following contributors:
layout by Q2A Media Services Pvt. Ltd.; audio production by Hart McLeod, Cambridge